TALES FROM THE
MIAMI HURRICANES
SIDELINE

A COLLECTION OF THE GREATEST
HURRICANE STORIES EVER TOLD

BY
JIM MARTZ

SPORTS
PUBLISHING

Sports Publishing books may be purchased in bulk at special discounts for sales promotion, corporate gifts, fund-raising, or educational purposes. Special editions can also be created to specifications. For details, contact the Special Sales Department, Sports Publishing, 307 West 36th Street, 11th Floor, New York, NY 10018 or sportspubbooks@skyhorsepublishing.com.

Sports Publishing® is a registered trademark of Skyhorse Publishing, Inc.®, a Delaware corporation.

Visit our website at www.sportspubbooks.com

10 9 8 7 6 5 4 3 2 1

Library of Congress Cataloging-in-Publication Data is available on file.

ISBN: 978-1-61321-223-3

Printed in the United States of America

To the Miami Hurricanes' family of players and coaches, whose commitment to excellence created the unprecedented success of the program.

CONTENTS

CHAPTER 1

Coming of Age

A STORM OVER "HURRICANES"

Before they were the Hurricanes, they were the no-names. The University of Miami played its first game in 1926 without a nickname. And once the name Hurricanes was adopted, it started a storm of controversy.

Tradition says Porter Norris, a member of the first football team, was the first to use the nickname Hurricanes. It caught on quickly, but there were detractors. And others have been opposed to the name over the years, most recently in 1992 after parts of South Florida were devastated by Hurricane Andrew.

School officials and local dignitaries originally wanted to name the team for local flora or fauna, but Norris said players wouldn't stand for that. Could you imagine the Miami Orange Blossoms? Or the Miami Ferns?

Norris suggested Hurricanes because the opening game had been postponed because of a hurricane. A few months into the first season, the *Miami Herald* reported that the name was offensive to many people in the area who felt all reference to hurricanes should be eliminated "in word and thought." A couple of weeks later the newspaper conceded that the name had not really been given. It had happened and probably could not be changed.

In the 1930s, an area journalist campaigned to get rid of the nickname because he felt it was bad public relations in the area's efforts to lure tourists and new development. But he gave up when students threatened to hang him—and not in effigy.

In 1960, Chicago financier and Florida real estate developer John D. MacArthur tried to stir up another effort to change the nickname.

"Shivers ran up and down my back every time when they mentioned the 'Hurricanes' during the telecast of the Miami-Pitt game last week," billionaire MacArthur complained. "Why keep reminding people there are Florida hurricanes? This hurricane business is played up beyond all proportions."

South Florida realtors and UM officials were not impressed with his reasoning. A university spokesman replied: "Does anyone think that Chicago is full of bears just because the town has a football team by that name?"

THREE GAMES IN EIGHT DAYS

In 1930, the Hurricanes played an ambitious schedule that included three road games in a span of just eight days. They also played in one of the first night games ever in the United States.

On October 31, the Hurricanes staged the first night game in the area at the new Moore Park stadium at Seventh Avenue and Thirty-Sixth Street near downtown Miami. The field was lighted by unprotected, high-watt bulbs, and longtime fans recalled that when it rained, exploding bulbs could be heard as the field gradually grew darker.

The three-game road trip began on November 8 against Temple University of Philadelphia and was played in the auditorium at Atlantic City, N.J. It was Miami's first intersectional game and was just the second college football game played indoors.

An estimated three million square feet of Pennsylvania black dirt was brought to the auditorium to make the grassless field. Bill Kimbrough, center on the team, recalled that "they had held a hockey game in the auditorium the night before and put this reddish brown substance—clay or whatever it was—over the frozen surface. Anyway, it was as hard as a rock."

Hurricane players brought coconuts to the game and gave them to the Temple players. Then Temple handed Miami a 34-0 defeat.

"The big teams frowned on night football then as such a commercial exhibition," said Wilbert Bach, Miami's first sports publicity man. "But Miami was struggling and saw a chance to pick up some money and grabbed it."

After the game the Hurricanes traveled to Dothan, Alabama, to play Howard the following Tuesday afternoon. The game was played in rain on a makeshift field. After the first two plays the players were covered with lime that burned through their jerseys and caused painful burns before the second half. The Hurricanes had no dry uniforms for a change at halftime, and the lime burns took a toll. After the game, which they lost 24-0, they headed for Lafayette, Louisiana, handicapped by the loss of several linemen and two backs. But they salvaged the trip with a 6-0 victory over Southwest Louisiana on Saturday.

SEE YOU LATER, GATORS

The long and often bitter rivalry with the University of Florida began with a bang for the Hurricanes and embarrassment for the host Gators in 1938. On the third game of the season before 5,000 fans, including 3,500 who came by train from Miami, coach Jack Hardings's fledgling team pulled off a stunning 19-7 victory.

"The Hurricanes breezed into Gainesville the morning of October 14," reported the school paper *The Ibis*, "behaved themselves that night, and the next evening, led by Captain Eddie Dunn and a fighting spirit, they promptly muzzled the surprised Gators."

Dunn scored all three touchdowns. Walt Kichefski, one of Miami's greatest ends who later became a Hurricane coach and gained a reputation as the all-time Gator hater, several years later fondly recalled playing that day in Gainesville.

"Florida had refused to play us until then," said Kichefski. "We were the young upstarts with big ideas and dreams and they looked down their noses at us. They were an all-boys school then and were more obnoxious than they are now. They were meaner than rattlesnakes. But when we walked off the field at the end of the game, their fans were as quiet as a graveyard at midnight."

Gator Week

Walt Kichefski never referred to the University of Florida as the Gators. To him they were "The Gator." Kichefski played end for the Hurricanes in the first game against Florida in 1938 and went on to serve as an assistant coach, interim head coach and head of the Athletic Federation. Every season during Gator week he would gather former players, alumni and fans along the sideline at practice to fire up the team for one more battle with "The Gator." He would remind them of how Florida looked with disdain at the little private school to the south. He'd recall the Gator Flop and all the other controversies that made this a heated rivalry.

"For several years, Walt used to have members of the '38 squad come out to practice during Gator Week to get them motivated," said his widow, Helene Kichefski. "They'd line up along the side, and some of them were rather plump and very much out of shape, but they had that old school spirit."

And each year Walt Kichefski would do his imitation of an alligator. "He'd shuffle his feet and snort like a gator," Helene said. "He'd have his elbows bent over like a walking gator. He couldn't wait for Gator week."

Helene Kichefski recalled that her husband's negative feelings toward the Gators increased when he became an assistant coach and handled most of the recruiting. "That's when his dislike for the Gator really grew," she said. "He'd run into them when he was recruiting. He'd have a good recruit and thought the player was sold on Miami, and he'd find out the Gators played up the Suntan U thing. It was hard to overcome that.

"But he had a lot of fun with it, too. He knew the coaches and was very fond of Ray Graves and Gene Ellison. I think in his last television interview at the UM Hall of Fame, he laughed and said it had been a lot of fun over the years."

It wasn't fun one day for Helene Kichefski and Marge Kalbac, the wife of the Hurricanes' team physician.

"One of the last games up there, I told Walt that the Gators seemed awfully nice and had toned down their antics and it should be a good, clean game," Helene Kichefski said. "Marge and I were standing under a staircase at the stadium waiting for our husbands before the game. All of a sudden some students dumped a bucket of ice on us. Walt said, 'They're nicer, eh?'"

Helene paused and added, "I'm looking at a gator right now that has Walt's name on it. It hangs by one of our lamps with a rope around its neck."

A HURRICANE AND A GATOR

Over the years, several high school recruits have announced that they would play with the Hurricanes and changed their minds and became Gators, or vice versa. But according to Jorge Milian of the *Palm Beach Post*, of the more than 3,000 players who have lettered at Miami and Florida, only two have lettered for both.

Phil Kaplan of Brooklyn, New York, was the first, playing for Florida in 1942 and for Miami in 1943 and 1946 as a two-way guard. He was in a class of his own until quarterback Brock Berlin transferred from Florida to Miami in 2002 and started for the Hurricanes in 2003. Both made the switch because they sought more playing time.

"When I graduated from high school I thought I had a scholarship to Cornell University and I wanted to be a veterinarian," recalls Kaplan. "Unfortunately my grades weren't that great and I wound up at South Carolina. Lo and behold, after a couple of weeks the coach said, 'I'd like to send you to junior college for some experience.' I went to Middle Georgia College for two years and went back home in the summer. A friend of mine had a scholarship to the University of Florida and said, 'Why don't you come with me?' and we both hitchhiked to Gainesville and I made the team and got a scholarship. We lost to Georgia 75-0 that year.

"When we came to play the University of Miami, the morning of the game I was enlisted into the navy. I was stationed in Miami."

After playing for the Hurricanes in 1943, Kaplan spent two years of active duty in the Pacific war zone in World War II.

"I came back in 1946 to the University of Florida, and the coach didn't want me so I came back to Miami," says Kaplan. "There were no transfer rules then that forced you to sit out a year. We played home games on Friday nights. That was the thing of the week. We played with leather helmets and no face masks."

Kaplan, who lives near the UM campus, met Berlin during a practice in the spring of 2003. "I said to him, 'You have to pay your dues. I'm the only member [of the Florida-to-Miami transfer club].'"

Berlin certainly paid his dues in his first home start—against his former Gator teammates in the Orange Bowl in

2003. He struggled in the first half but led the Hurricanes to a rousing comeback and turned boos into cheers, completing 19 of his last 22 passes as Miami overcame a 33-10 deficit and won 38-33.

"I'm just so thankful I'm here at Miami and part of such a great program, around great coaches and teammates," said Berlin.

And which team did Kaplan cheer for?

"I root for Florida when they're not playing Miami," he said. "But I want Miami to win. I live and die with them."

UNHAPPY IN GAINESVILLE

Don Mariutto Sr. didn't stay at Florida long enough to letter and ended up becoming a standout guard for the Hurricanes.

"A unique thing that happened my freshman year was that I went to Florida and I wasn't real happy with the place," recalls Mariutto of the 1949 season. "I called down to a friend at Miami, Charlie George, and told him to call coach Andy Gustafson. Andy said to Charlie, 'Tell him we'll take him back.' I didn't finish my freshman year and played only two games. I didn't letter and played on the freshman team."

Mariutto thinks it's interesting that he and Kaplan and Berlin all transferred from Florida to Miami. "We've never lost a player that I know of to Florida," he adds. "That's got to say something."

AIRPORT RUNWAY MADNESS

The 1950 season can be called the year the Hurricanes came of age and the first time their fans went wild. The highlight

Don Mariutto

was a 20-14 victory at Purdue one week after the Boilermakers ended Notre Dame's unbeaten streak at 39 games. It is generally considered the school's biggest victory in its first 55 seasons, and it touched off a raucous three-day celebration back in South Florida.

The team had two quarterbacks—Jack (Mr. Short Pass) Hackett and Bob (Mr. Long Pass) Schneidenbach. Hackett, better known as Mighty Mouse, barely weighed 140 pounds and one foot was two inches shorter than the other because of polio. He was the star of the upset of Purdue. The team also featured running back Harry "The Scooter" Mallios, who later became Miami's athletic director.

While Purdue was knocking off the Irish, the Hurricanes defeated Villanova 18-12 in the Orange Bowl. But Villanova coach Jim Leonard wasn't impressed. "Purdue will slaughter Miami, but you should do well with everyone else."

At West Lafayette, Indiana, the Hurricanes overcame a 7-0 deficit and scored all 20 of their points in the second half.

"We were beaten by a more aggressive team," said Purdue coach Stu Holcomb. "Our squad was in the doldrums."

And the Hurricanes were in the clouds. "I believe our line whipped Purdue's line, and that probably is the real answer to the ball game," said coach Andy Gustafson.

The United Press International account of the game called it an upset "that was equally as staggering as last week's downfall of the Irish."

An estimated 100,000 people tried to greet the team at Miami International Airport when it returned the next day, including 30,000 who surged through police barricades set up hastily at the airport to meet the team's chartered plane, the Dreadnaught.

The plane had to circle the field several times while police begged the crowd to clear the runway. Thousands more sat in cars trapped in a traffic jam backed up two miles.

A police motorcade led the team out of the airport gate and down Flagler Street to Bayfront Park in downtown Miami for a rally at the amphitheater.

Said the *Miami Herald*: "Miami, that allegedly sophisticated resort city, took down her hair, threw off her corset and broke into a college cheer Sunday when her football team came home with Purdue's treasured scalp.... The town was one big noise, a noise halfway between a million automobile horns and a thousand cow bells, all going at the same time. Even the prisoners from the 16th to 25th floors of the courthouse were tossing out confetti, homemade out of toilet tissue."

THE LITTLE TEAM THAT COULD

"The victory at Purdue was unbelievable," recalled Don Mariutto Sr., a Hurricanes lineman in the early 1950s. "Here was this little school from Miami. We were not really considered a national team. We had played some Big Ten and Southeastern Conference teams but were never in that league like we were much later.

"It was unreal when we won. The fans in the stands and players on the field field went crazy. Then with over 100,000 waiting at the airport, we had to circle the field several times for them to clear the runway. We had a tickertape parade in convertibles all the way downtown to Bayfront Park. The streets were lined all the way, we couldn't get cars out of the airport, we didn't expect that. Miami had gone wild.

"Coach Andy Gustafson got the keys to the city. And in a newspaper article in California, the reporter wrote that now he was convinced college football was under the grasp of gamblers, because there was no way Miami could legitimately win at Purdue."

Mariutto added, "We went on to play in the Orange Bowl. Unfortunately we lost by 15-14 to Clemson when Harry Mallios was tackled in end zone for a safety.

"Andy had a little problem drinking once in a while, and I remember after the Orange Bowl game at the banquet we got Universal Geneva watches, and Andy was at the podium making an acceptance speech and he dropped a couple of them. The next day we all had to go get our watches and didn't want the ones he had dropped. I still have my watch, and it's still running."

CANOE STAYS AFLOAT

In 1955, the city of Hollywood, Florida, donated an authentic Seminole war canoe as a trophy for the annual Miami-Florida game. The six-foot-long canoe was hand carved and painted by Seminole Indians from a 200-year-old Everglades cypress tree felled by lightning.

For several years it was a cherished prize, similar to the Little Brown Jug that goes to the winner of the Michigan-Minnesota game or the Old Oaken Bucket that goes to the Indiana-Purdue winner. A Seminole would stand guard during the Miami-Florida game, and the winning team would carry the canoe around the field. Then the canoe would be displayed on the campus of the winning team until the next season.

For a while it became a symbol of the Hurricanes-Gator series and promoted the city of Hollywood. But instead of becoming an enduring memento, the canoe eventually gathered dust in closets. Florida often stored it in a Florida Field maintenance shed.

Norm Carlson, Florida's assistant athletic director, recalled that after one game in the 1970s, "it was raining. A Seminole Indian stood there on the sidelines, waiting for the presentation ceremony. But there were some mixed signals, and nobody showed. The stadium was emptying, the field was deserted, and that Indian just stood there, looking for somebody to come get the canoe."

Former Hurricane lineman Don Marriutto Sr. recalled that the canoe was missing for several years and nobody was sure if it was in Coral Gables or Gainesville. Then one day in the 1970s, Mariutto and Walt Kichefski literally stumbled across history.

"We would work out at the Hecht building on campus Monday through Friday at 7 a.m. and walk three to four miles and reminisce about the old times and solve all the world's problems," said Mariutto. "One day we walked past this big pile of junk ready for the normal Coral Gables pick up. There was a new coaching regime—maybe it was in Carl Selmer's days. It's hard to remember because coaches were coming and going [Miami had seven head coaches in the 1970s, including Kichefski on an interim basis].

"It simply wasn't the way things were done around here at the time. There was a continual revolving door and no tradition at all. We decided to try to salvage the tradition."

Mariutto said there was old film, footballs from the 1930s and 1940s, programs, yearbooks and a stone football statue laying in a trash pile. "We couldn't salvage all of it," he noted. "But we did see the canoe. It was bigger than Walter could handle at his house, and it had a big plaque on the canoe. He took the plaque and I took the canoe. I said I'd hold onto it until somebody appreciated it again.

"My sister-in-law decided to paint it. It was a mahogany tree canoe and was a priceless piece of work done by the Indians. It floated in my pool several years and sometimes we'd take it out. We'd have fund-raising parties for the old Athletic Foundation, which was the forerunner of the Hurricane Club, and we'd invite prospective people who could support the foundation. And we'd tell them the story about the canoe.

"There were several articles wondering what happened to the canoe. We'd chuckle and keep quiet. Finally the Kearns Hall of Fame building was built for the University of Miami Sports Hall of Fame and now there was a place for it, and it came out of hiding. My sister's paint job was removed, to her dismay, and the original mahogany was restored and it's displayed at the hall. I don't know whether Florida ever made claims for it. Apparently we were the last to win it before it disappeared."

Friday Nights

D on Mariutto Sr. recalls that it was Miami's tradition for many seasons in the 1950s and '60s and into the early '70s to play on Friday nights.

"The thought was that it was too hot in the afternoon and there was no television coverage and we got prime recognition on the radio. And on Saturday morning we got good press coverage.

"The only thing we had to compete with was high school football, and most of the games in Miami were played on Thursday night. Miami High sometimes played on Saturday nights, and at certain points the Stingarees would outdraw the University of Miami. One year we played Jackson and drew 37,000, and that was more than any UM game that year. High school football was very big and there were very few schools in Miami, including Edison and Coral Gables and Miami Beach. Miami High didn't lose to another area school in 37 years."

Dr. Harry Mallios, who played for the Hurricanes in the 1950s and was athletic director from 1979-83, recalled that former ticket director Art Lasky said, "The reason we played on Fridays was because no teams played then, and the newspapers would pick up the game, and it publicized the program up north."

As the population grew and more high schools played on Fridays, the Friday-night tradition ended in 1972, returned in 1973, except for the Notre Dame and Florida games, and was abandoned for good in 1974.

SNOW JOB IN KENTUCKY

Dr. Mallios remembers a wild trip to play at Kentucky in 1951.

"We used to take Pan American Airways as our team carrier," he said. "The flight to Lexington, Kentucky, left on a Friday morning for a Saturday afternoon game. As we approached Kentucky, the weather really turned nasty. I was sitting in a window seat and the plane was in its landing approach.

As we got lower and lower, it was snowing harder and harder. I was looking for landing lights or rooftops covered with snow. We had an old-time captain, and for some reason or other, the engines revved up very high and resulted in the plane going into a steep climb. I saw a large object just below the wing. A teammate said, 'Did you see that?' It was a huge cross at the peak of a church steeple. With the steep climb the captain said, 'Sorry fellas, we cannot land due to the weather. We have clearance to land in Indianapolis.'

"We were met by busses and it took several hours to get to Lexington. We had no workout at the stadium. And that may have been a sign of the nature of how the game would go. We were an 8-3 team and were invited to the Gator Bowl. It was cold in Lexington, and we were trounced, 32-0."

Going into the game the Hurricanes were ranked 14th and the Wildcats were 19th. Kentucky's quarterback was the fabled Babe Parelli.

"We were watching him during pregame warmups," Mallios said. "We noticed he kept putting his hands into his jersey. It was really cold, but we thought we should have it easy if he's cold. On the contrary, we were the ones to get cold hands. He had hand warmers in his jersey. We were Southern boys and were not familiar with such things as hand warmers."

"M" Club Initiation

Dr. Mallios has vivid memories of the initiation into the old "M" Club, the lettermen's club.

"Following the 1950 season, we met in the courtyard of the old Cardboard College," he said. "The football locker room was on the first floor. We would dress in full gear and walk down to the practice field about a block and a half away at what now is called the French Village, where Coral Gables Youth Center now sits.

Harry Mallios

"We inductees were told we had to jog from Cardboard College to the main campus where the bookstore is. And we were pretty well bushed when we got there. Then we had to jump in the canal east of the school of business, swim across the 30-foot canal, break off a palm from the small palms, and swim back across while holding the palms.

"The big linemen were really bushed. One lineman, Ted Buoyoucas—we called him Buckets for short—was one of the last to arrive. He had flat feet. He jumped in with everyone else and made a mad dash to find a palm frond and hold it overhead and swim back. Halfway back he was struggling, and he was not an especially good swimmer. He started go down, and someone jumped in to help him. He nearly went down for the count."

WHO'S THE GRAY-HAIRED GUY?

D r. Mallios, an academic advisor to athletes for several years, has another vivid memory:

"On away games when I played in the 1950s we were bussed to the airport from the fieldhouse. The official parties were already on board in first class when we got to the plane. One distinguished gray-haired guy was sitting there and I asked coach Andy Gustafson, 'Who is the gray-haired guy?' He said, 'Harry, come with me.' We went up to first class and he said, 'Harry, I want you to meet Dr. Bowman Ashe, the president of the university.' You can imagine my embarrassment. Dr. Ashe asked where I was from and what was my academic interest. I was so happy to meet him. He was a great visionary and really was the father of the university. He was a wonderful man, so calm, so pleasant. My position coach, Eddie Dunn, married his daughter."

CHAPTER 2

Gotham, Matador and Mad Stork

NEVER MIND

Andy Gustafson had the longest tenure of any head football coach at Miami, 16 seasons beginning in 1948 and ending after George Mira's senior season in 1963.

"I just loved Gus," longtime *Miami Herald* sports editor Edwin Pope recalled. "He was a wonderful guy. When I first came down here I covered the University of Florida. I got to know Gus after 1956. He was in Alcoholics Anonymous and loved to tell me the story about his brother, who said, 'When you feel your worst, look your best.' Gus told me he had this horrible hangover and came in the office at six in morning as he usually did, dressed up in a suit. After a while he couldn't stand wearing it any more. He got in his car and drove out to an old, well-known hangout out by Tropical Park race track. He figured at 6:30 in the morning there was no way anybody was going to recognize him. He put on his dark sunglasses and pulled his cap down over his eyes and sat down at the bar. He said, 'Scotch and soda, please.' The bartender said, 'Coming right up, Coach!' Gus didn't bother to have a drink and went back to office."

Andy Gustafson

THE GOTHAM BOWL

Only the most ardent trivia buffs would know the answer to this question: What was the Gotham Bowl and where was it played?

It was a short-lived college football bowl game in the House That Ruth Built, Yankee Stadium in New York City. And Miami played in the second annual game in 1962, though there was concern that the game would even be played.

When the Hurricanes defeated Florida 17-15 in the final game of the 1962 season, they received bids to the Gator Bowl and the Gotham Bowl. They chose New York with its flashing lights, Broadway theaters and Yankee Stadium. What they got was a newspaper strike, a poorly promoted game and sub-freezing temperatures.

The opponent was Nebraska, and both teams threatened not to show up because they hadn't received contracts and feared the Gotham Bowl wouldn't cover expenses. Fifteen minutes before the deadline set by Miami president Dr. Henry King Stanford, New York's Mayor Wagner called to say that $30,000 in expenses had been placed in an escrow account.

Though both teams showed up, only 6,166 spectators attended the game that was played in 17-degree weather at ice-covered and snow-banked Yankee Stadium. There was no national television, which meant the country missed a wild contest in which the lead changed hands six times before Nebraska won 36-34.

Miami quarterback George Mira had perhaps his finest game, completing 24 passes for 321 yards and two touchdowns. The press said he was the greatest passer to appear at Yankee Stadium since Notre Dame's Johnny Lujack in the 1940s.

THE MATADOR

George Mira Sr., the Hurricanes' first All-America quarterback, went 2-1 against Florida in his three years as a starter (1961-63).

"That was THE game," he said. "We always looked forward to it. It made our season. The big reason was that a lot of

George Mira

the guys at Florida [were guys] I played with and against in high school.

"It was a lot stronger rivalry than it was against Florida State, probably because we played Florida longer."

Mira, known as "The Matador" because of his elusiveness, was the hero of Miami's 17-15 victory over Florida in 1962 when he threw a left-handed pass (he was right-handed) for the winning touchdown at Gainesville.

"We had marched down to their 10-yard line," Mira said. "We called a play action to the left. The defensive end came off his block and grabbed my waist. My right arm was locked underneath and I flipped the ball to my left hand—I don't know what made me do it. I saw Nick Spinelli alone in the end zone and threw it to him."

HIRED AT A FUNERAL

When Andy Gustafson retired after the 1963 season, Miami officials wanted a big-name coach and interviewed Nebraska's Bob Devaney; former Miami assistant Hank Stram, who was coach at the Dallas team that became the Kansas City Chiefs in the AFL; and Northwestern's Ara Parseghian, who cancelled a meeting and took the job at Notre Dame. Miami ended up hiring Charlie Tate, a Georgia Tech assistant who had won four state titles in five years at Miami Senior High School.

Miami's board of trustees selected Tate in a meeting at a Sunday school room following a funeral.

"One of our trustees, Daniel H. Redfeard, had died, and the funeral was to be in the United First Methodist Church of Coral Gables," said University of Miami president Dr. Henry King Stanford. "It occurred to me that if all the athletic committee members of the board were going to be at the funeral, we would save everybody another trip by meeting after the funeral. We met in a Sunday school room, and Tate was elected coach."

Mad Stork Stalks Spurrier

Longtime assistant coach Walt Kichefski's prized pupil was Ted "The Mad Stork" Hendricks, a three-time All-America defensive end in the mid-1960s. One of Hendricks's golden moments as a Hurricane came in the 21-16 upset of Florida at Gainesville in 1966. Hendricks hounded Gator quarterback and eventual Heisman Trophy winner Steve Spurrier throughout the game.

Hendricks recalled that it was "a very bitter rivalry," one that carried over into the NFL.

"We played them the last game of the season in 1966 and he hadn't won the Heisman Trophy yet," said Hendricks, who went onto a legendary NFL career with the Oakland Raiders. "We forced him to throw early—not only me but the other end, Phil Smith. We kept hastening his throw and sacking him all game long.

"He carried animosity toward me throughout his pro career. I remember harassing him in a game when he was with the Tampa Bay Bucs. I jumped up to block a pass and he aimed it at my midsection."

Jump Ball Offense

Hendricks was six foot eight and 220 pounds, and Kichefski estimated that a leaping Hendricks presented a 14-foot obstacle for a quarterback to throw over. Hendricks also present-ed a 14-foot target to throw to. And that got coaches to think-ing about putting Hendricks at offensive end as well as defen-sive end during the 1968 season.

"We're going to try to help Hendricks get the Heisman

Ted Hendricks chases Steve Spurrier.

Trophy by using him at offensive end in certain situations," said coach Charlie Tate during spring practice.

So Tate created the Jump Ball Offense on the goal line with Hendricks, six-foot-four Ray Bellamy and six-foot-three Dave Kalima in the lineup. The quarterback would fire the ball high in the end zone, and the receivers would try to win the jump ball.

But Hendricks suffered a chest injury and missed the spring game. And the Jump Ball Offense was used only once— late in the fourth quarter of a 28-7 victory over Northwestern in the opening game.

"If we had to beat teams by 28 points to get in our Jump Ball Offense, I saw no future in that," said Hendricks.

Tate, who wasn't pleased with his quarterbacks, added: "Having a pro offense like ours with great receivers but no first-rate quarterback is like having a new limousine with a chimpanzee at the wheel."

Coach Vanishes During Season

For convenience in the 1970s, UM officials could have installed a revolving door at the head football coach's office. The Hurricanes answered to seven different head coaches that decade.

As Jonathan Rand of the *Miami News* wrote, when Howard Schnellenberger moved into his office in January, 1979, "He probably found curtains put up by Fran Curci, rugs laid by Pete Elliott, pictures hung by Carl Selmer and furniture put in by Lou Saban. It seemed there was always a moving van in front of the Hecht Athletic Center."

The merry-go-round began in 1970 when Charlie Tate quit after just the second game of the season. In the opener, the Hurricanes whipped William and Mary 36-14 before just 27,286 at the Orange Bowl, the smallest opening crowd since 1953. Meanwhile the Dolphins, in their first season under Don Shula, drew 57,140. The next week at Georgia Tech, Miami was upset 31-21. On the following Tuesday, Tate resigned as coach and athletic director effective immediately.

He did not attend the press conference and wasn't available for comment but left a statement saying he resigned "in the best interest of the university and its athletic program." He had a 34-27-3 record and was in the last year of his contract.

Tate vanished from the public for five days, then was interviewed in Jacksonville at his brother Buddy's home.

"I haven't been hiding from anyone," he said. "I'm just trying to collect my thoughts. I just got tired of the job. I thought I might be better off somewhere else."

Several weeks later he revealed that his wife and three sons had been harassed by obscene phone calls, defilement of his yard with a load of manure and vandalism of his car. He also cited a lack of communication between the administration and the athletic department and reiterated his frustration with pro football. He went on to be an assistant coach of the New Orleans Saints and small-town high schools in Florida and was head coach of the Jacksonville Sharks in the short-lived World Football League.

FINDING CHARLIE TATE

Edwin Pope, the *Miami Herald's* longtime sports editor, remembered Tate's disappearance as well.

"He just vanished," Pope recalled. "And two days later Eddie Storin, the *Herald's* executive sports editor, came in the office and said, 'OK, Edwin, we're going to find Charlie Tate.' So we got in a car and started driving up through the state. We both knew he had a lot of connections throughout the state. George Trogdon, the famous Miami High coach who'd worked for Charlie, had some orange groves up by Leesburg. We found his little house out in the orange groves and started talking to George and he was talking about how horrible it was about Charlie. We kept badgering him, and he said, 'I haven't heard from Charlie, but he's good friends with a guy who owns a sporting goods store in Leesburg.' At nine or 10 at night we found him there. He looked very crestfallen, and he said, 'I guess you found me.' We went to a Holiday Inn and he poured his soul out.

Charlie Tate

"He said people had knocked in the trunk of his car with a tire iron and dumped manure on his lawn. As pigheaded as he was, he couldn't stand any criticism. We asked him if he had any money. 'No, I don't have any money.' He said he had a little Farm Store that he made a little money in. He was in the depths.

"That's the only time in my life that I've known of a college football coach leaving during the season. I've done the research and I've never heard of a guy doing that. So you knew he was desperate.

"One thing that got him down was the Miami Dolphins. It quickly became apparent when the Dolphins started their franchise in the late 1960s that people were going to go crazy over them. Charlie said, 'They're in the paper 365 days a year and nobody mentions us 'til the middle of August, and they never talk about us after the season.' That's what did him in. He went on to a strange career with the Jacksonville Sharks in the old USFL. I remember one night before a Sharks game, his son was a quarterback somewhere and was about five foot nine. I said, 'That's not very tall,' and he got very angry. He was always ready to fight. He said, 'How tall do you have to be?'"

A HURRICANE TIGER GROWLS

Armand "Stitch" Vari, a Hurricane lineman from 1950-52 and an assistant coach for several years, remembers the time when longtime assistant Walt Kichefski was getting the team ready to play LSU in Baton Rouge in the early 1960s.

"He told the players that LSU is a very well-coached football team, but we are well coached, too," Vari recalled. "He said, 'LSU's team mascot is Mike, a live tiger in a cage equipped with a microphone. When we run out onto the playing field an LSU cheerleader will run past Mike's cage wielding a stick. Then all 68,000 LSU fans will let loose and growl and roar along with the raging tiger.'

"With that, Walt, who was lying flat on his side on his desk with a hand on his head, growled loudly in imitation of the tiger. Then the players all joined in and they were ready to play."

The Hurricanes gave the sixth-ranked Tigers a battle before bowing 17-3.

MORE KICHEFSKI TALES

Helene Kichefski, widow of Walt Kichefski and an avid Hurricane fan, recalls that her husband often had the bed-check duty to make sure players were in their rooms before curfew. "Walt would always take our springer spaniel with medal ID tags and send the dog ahead to alert the boys he was coming."

Helene relates this story that Walt often told: "He was very proud of his Polish heritage. In the early years he did 95 percent of our recruiting. One time he was in Tennessee and checking into a motel. The young girl at the reception desk said, 'Are you married? What is your wife's maiden name?' He said, 'Putnam.' She shook her head and said, 'How could a name like that marry a name like this?'"

Walt literally ate and slept Hurricanes football. As Helene recalled, a fan gave him a birthday present of two white pillow cases with a big split "U" logo in orange and green on them. "He had two feather pillows and he'd put his head between them."

FRASER MEETS MIRA

During his 30-year career as head baseball coach at Miami (1963-92), Ron Fraser became known as The Wizard of College Baseball. His teams made an NCAA-record 20 consecutive postseason appearances and eight trips to the College World Series, winning national championships in 1982 and 1985.

His first season at Miami also was the year All-America quarterback George Mira was finishing his career. One day soon after Fraser arrived, he strolled behind the decaying dugout to find out who was throwing the ball so hard in a game of catch.

Fraser, having been away from the college football scene for three years, didn't recognize Mira.

"You pitch baseball?" Fraser asked.

Mira, who was a star at Key West High and almost signed a pro baseball contract with the Baltimore Orioles before enrolling at UM, said he had before going to college. In fact, Mira had compiled a 31-2 record and thrown two no-hitters while leading Key West to two Class A state titles.

"You throw harder than anybody I've got," said Fraser. "Say, how would you ..."

A reporter was standing nearby and revealed the incident in the newspaper the next day, exposing Fraser's hopes of turning Mira into a baseball star. But a few hours after the newspaper was delivered, football coach Andy Gustafson called Fraser into his office and presented a list to him of football players who were "free to play baseball, too."

Mira's name was not on the list.

"I got the message," said Fraser.

THE YAMMA YAMMA MAN

Cheerleading may be more dangerous than playing on the field. At least it was for Jim Fleming, a Hurricane cheerleader for four decades. No, it didn't take him that long to earn his degree. Fleming, a.k.a. the Yamma Yamma Man, was a cheerleader during his student days from 1964-68, and as an alumnus he grew into the role of firing up the crowd.

The job had its price, though. He dislocated both shoulders, ruptured an Achilles, broke his clavicle and suffered a concussion.

"They were passing me up the aisle, and nobody caught me and I got a concussion," recalled Fleming, who was president of the student body and founder of the campus radio station WVUM. "At the USC game here in 1966, I was doing a flip and landed the wrong way and dislocated my shoulder falling over a cheerleader. The USC doctor put it back in place in their locker room at halftime."

"At Florida in my first away game, I was the guy who carried all the flags. They were on long wooden dowels and were heavy. After the game I was lugging them up the ramp at the stadium and three guys accosted me. They dislocated my shoulder and kicked the heck out of me. They took the flags and set them on fire. Eventually the campus cops got them, and I spent the night in Shands Hospital."

Then there was the 0-0 game against Notre Dame in the Orange Bowl in 1965 in which he escaped injury in a confrontation with Fighting Irish coach Ara Parseghian. "We were obnoxious, and it was a highly charged atmosphere. In those days the students were behind the opponent's bench, and it was our job to get on the nerves of the opposing players and coaches and make them feel uncomfortable, like a road basketball game. We were doing a thing with the band, 'Cheer up Ara, the worst is yet to come.' And saying 'Aaaarra! Aaaarra!' By the third quarter, he'd had it. He came over to to me and said something you can't print. He said, 'Listen you little SOB. Shut up!' He grabbed me by the throat a little. He was hot. His veins were popping. It shocked me. Somebody was trying to restrain Ara and cool him down. This was before the Woody Hayes thing (when the Ohio State coach punched an opposing player). Times were different then. Then the kids went nuts. I was an extension of them, and they became personal after that with anti-Ara cheers."

BANNED IN MIAMI

Fleming went to an all-male Jesuit high school in Rochester, New York, "so I became a cheerleader and ran track and cross country. I was doing the things short guys do. At Miami they had a tryout for cheerleaders and I was mic man, just as I was in New York. I had the experience. I'd go in the stands and introduce myself. I was performing for my friends. We tried to be a unit, because we were behind the opponent's bench. I think we played a role in rattling the opposition.

"I got the reputation of being kind of a smart alec, a Jimmy Cageny character. Mickey Rooney with a chip on his shoulder. When John Routh was the Ibis, we matched so beautifully. We were both irreverent. My irreverence got me in trouble a lot of times.

"One time we were beating the pulp out of Pitt, 49-0 in the third quarter in the 1960s. It was very difficult to do that job when we were beating the heck out of the other team and everybody is bored. We started doing cheers for Pittsburgh. The kids in the stands yelled, 'Go, Panthers, go. Go to hell.' I wasn't leading them, but I was down there, and I got fingered for starting it. UM president Henry King Stanford sat me down for a game. It was my fault for leading cheers for the opposition and they started getting raunchy.

"There were a number of cheers back then that would be banned today as people have become more politically correct. We had one in which we said, 'Go bananas, go go bananas' in a strip-tease motion. Or we'd say, 'Hey, your momma ...' when there was a bad call or dirty play. They banned that one. It was all part of the Hurricane mystique. Another one was, 'Grind 'em in the dirt, mash 'em in the mud, we want blood.' That was also banned. In the '60s and '70s we could get away with that. They had one before I got there, that was stupid and filthy, I banned that one."

Fleming said this one about the Florida Gators was not banned: "Alligator bags, alligator shoes. If you're a Gator, you're born to lose."

IT'S A RIOT

Fleming even got arrested during a game in 1969, "and I probably deserved it. After I graduated, there was a stint in which I wanted to sit in the stands and watch the game. I was in the section next to the students. And the students, not being pleased with the current cheerleaders, carried me down to the field and the other cheerleaders would hand me the mic.

"The peanut vendors were all buddies of mine, and they said, 'We want to do Yamma with you.' They would do a conga line, then the soda venders came on down and soon the sidelines were filled. They were like lemmings coming over the railing in waves. Everybody started hounding me, saying, 'Why can't I be down there?' I said, 'Come on down. So the students and all the band came down to the sidelines. They had to hold up the game and called a 15-yard penalty for unsportsmanlike conduct. The cops came down and grabbed me and took me out of the stadium and put me in a paddy wagon. Kids were running after cops. I was charged with inciting a riot and disorderly conduct. Henry King Stanford came over and said, 'I'm the president of the university and he's just doing what he normally does.' And he told me to never do that again."

CHAPTER 3

The Revolving Door

THE INFAMOUS GATOR FLOP

One of the rare times in which one team purposely allowed another to score happened late in the 1971 season when the 4-5 Hurricanes met the 3-7 Florida Gators in the Orange Bowl. It's widely referred to as the Gator Flop.

Leading 45-8 and with Florida fans screaming, "Let them score!" the Gators literally flopped to the field and allowed Miami quarterback John Hornibrook to score a touchdown from eight yards out so Florida quarterback John Reaves would have a last minute shot at the NCAA career major-college passing record held by Stanford's Jim Plunkett.

Florida recovered the Hurricanes' onside kick, and Reaves, after nearly being intercepted, completed a 15-yard pass to surpass Plunkett's career total of 7,546 yards.

After the game, Miami coach Fran "The Little General" Curci refused to congratulate Florida coach Doug Dickey. Curci headed straight for the locker room and said, "It was the worst thing I have ever seen in football. I used to admire Doug Dickey as a coach—his record speaks for itself. But tonight I lost all respect for him as a coach and a man. What he did shows absolutely no class."

Curci added: "There was enough time left (1:10) for Florida to get the ball back legitimately and give him another chance. ... I know I would never do a disgraceful thing like that to anybody. College football is fighting for its life [against the pros] and can't stand acts like this. Actually, I feel sorry for Doug Dickey. I think he made a fool of himself. If he thinks that's the spirit of the game, he's got a long way to go."

Dickey, who was called before college football's ethics committee to explain what happened, said, "I would rather not have had to do it that way. But certain records are worth going after, I guess. I did not mean to embarrass the Miami football team in any way. I certainly did not give our kids instructions to fall down like that. I was a little disappointed they did."

In those days, there was a pond just beyond the east end zone where dolphins would swim during Miami Dolphins games. In a wild postgame celebration, the Gators jumped into the pond (there were no dolphins in it), heaving Reaves with them.

The Gator Flop

In the aftermath, Florida's University Athletic Association passed a resolution praising Dickey's decision. And Dickey would not second-guess himself.

"It didn't look to me like we were going to get the ball back any other way," he said. "And I felt in the best interest of our players I should try to help John Reaves. ... Whether our guys stand around and play grab on the play or whether they lie down is immaterial, in my opinion."

Said Curci: "He was passing against a crippled team, and Dickey knew this. The only healthy man in our defensive backfield was Burgess Owens. No, Dickey knew he had us down, and he took advantage of it to kick the hell out of a crippled team."

WINNING ON A FIFTH DOWN

Early in the 1972 season, the Hurricanes inadvertently became embroiled in another controversy when they defeated Tulane 24-21 thanks to an obvious fifth-down play.

With 54 seconds remaining and fourth down showing on the official NCAA play by play for the second time, Ed Carney threw a 32-yard pass to Witt Beckman for the winning touchdown in the Orange Bowl. On fourth and 24, Carney had thrown incomplete and UM players started off the field, but officials called them back and said it was fourth down, though it actually was fifth. Officials later denied they had made a mistake.

The next day, Tulane president Herbert E. Longenecker urged UM to forfeit the game. UM officials and board of trustees members met in a "soul-searching" meeting and, with the strong backing of the NCAA Rules Committee, announced forfeiture would be inappropriate because Tulane still had a minute to score and change the outcome.

CAIN WAS ABLE

Though the Hurricanes managed only two winning seasons in the 1970s (6-5 in 1974 and 1978), players found ways to keep their spirits up with the usual college pranks. Larry Cain, a speedy wingback from 1973-76, remembers those days well.

"When Ruben Carter, an All-Amcrica defensive lineman, was in school with us, we'd put hot sauce in his fruit punch," he said. "A lot of us were sitting at the training table saying, 'Who's going to do it?' We were scared to do it, so I talked quarterback Frank Glover into doing it. Rubin drank his drink and spit it out and started looking around and looked right at me and I started running. Then he looked at Frank, who said, 'I didn't do it.'

"You didn't mess with Ruben. When they moved me to varsity, after one week I went into the slot. I was the up-back on the punts, and Ruben was right over me. We were both from Fort Lauderdale and I thought, 'This is my home boy, and he's going to take it easy.' I went for his knees, and the next thing I knew he blocked me all the way back into the punter.

"The following year running back Taylor Timmons, whose nickname was Goo Goo Rock, came in and we told him the initiation to the team was to put hot sauce in Eddie Edwards's drink. Edwards, another All-America defensive lineman, went crazy and said, 'I'm going to kill the dude who did this.' He chased Taylor out the door with a hamburger in his hand.

"One night I did something to Frank Glover. Frank and Mike Adams (a defensive back) knocked on my door at 2 o'clock in the morning. I didn't know who it was. I opened the door and this big bucket of water spilled into my room, and I knew right away who did it. So, I put two garbage cans above their door, knocked on their door and set off the fire alarm and got them back good.

"Then one time my roommate Dicki Hall and I were walking by Lake Osceola by the old band room, we had some balloons filled with water and waited for Frank and Mike to walk by. Mike took off and we saw Frank behind the bushes and got him and disappeared into the night."

Cain and several other Hurricanes were members of Omega Psi Phi fraternity, and naturally that meant more pranks. "Ernie Jones, Mike Adams, and my brother Nate were defensive backs, and they were my big brothers while we were pledging. In practice we'd have to block them and catch balls. Against Ernie I beat him bad, and he said, 'You're making me look bad. Wait until tonight.' That night we had to answer certain history questions and they'd make us pay for it. The next day at practice I started dropping balls and missing assignments. I said, 'I don't know, Coach, I just missed it.' I'd run away from them. One day I told Coach I was pledging, and all the DBs were going to get me."

In the 1970s, Notre Dame dominated its rivalry with Miami as the teams met annually, and Cain made good friends with Fighting Irish star defensive back Luther Bradley. "I went out for a pass and Luther was right there," said Cain. "He's about 6-2 and very intimidating. The next time I tried to block him he grabbed me and said, 'The next time you do this, I'll blind you.' The next time I beat him for 62 yards and ran for a touchdown. I turned and rolled the dice to him. After the game he said, 'That's the first time I've been beaten like that. You want to go to a party?' Ever since then we've been great friends. I represented him in the USFL. I was his agent."

THE FUNKY CHICKEN

At the opening of the 1976 season, the second under Carl Selmer, tailback Ottis Anderson and wingback Larry Cain punctuated their touchdowns by doing the Funky Chicken in the end zone during a 47-0 victory over Florida State and its new coach, Bobby Bowden.

"We got together before bed check the night before the game and went over our choreography," said Cain.

One dance, "The Muscle," simply meant flexing your arms. For another, called "Rolling Six," Cain would kneel and roll the ball like dice. He also considered doing the splits but feared he would pull a hamstring. This was long before end-zone theatrics became popular in the NFL and were banned in college football.

Selmer did not disapprove of the actions, which gained national attention when the *Miami Herald* ran a feature with a picture of Anderson dancing and slapping hands with quarterback E.J. Baker. The story ran under the headline: "UM Campaign Promise: Chicken in Every End Zone."

Colorado coach Bill Mallory saw a copy of the story before the Hurricanes visited Boulder the next week and put it on the bulletin board in the team's dressing room.

"They ain't jigging in my damn end zone," Mallory grumbled.

And they didn't. The Hurricanes never got close to the end zone in a 33-3 loss. And the Funky Chicken disappeared in a 3-8 season that ended with Selmer's dismissal.

THANKS, COACH

Long before Jerome Brown, Russell Maryland and Warren Sapp became superstar defensive linemen at Miami, the Hurricanes developed several All-America defensive linemen under the tutelage of longtime assistant Harold Allen. They included Tony Cristiani, Rubin Carter, Eddie Edwards, Don Latimer, Don Smith, Lester Williams and Jim Burt. Former assistant coach and player Bill Trout remembers this story about Gary Dunn, a standout from 1973-75 who was a *National Independent* first-team tackle.

"When Gary was drafted by the Pittsburgh Steelers in 1976, they were the most dominant team then," Trout said. "They had a tremendous defensive line led by Mean Joe Green. Gary was sort of down in the dumps, though, saying, 'How will I ever make this team?'

"He was working out in Miami and he sees Harold Allen. Harold says, 'What's wrong?' Dunn said, 'I've been drafted by the Steelers, and I could never fill Joe Green's jockstrap.' Allen replied, 'They drafted you for a purpose. You come from a good program, you're strong, you have good speed and you're a competitor.' Harold started to walk away and turned back and said, 'Oh, and by the way, you can't fill Joe Green's jockstrap.'"

TIME FOR A CHANGE

You know it's time to change coaches, or at least your offense, when fans in the stands know what plays you're going to run next. That's what Miami vice president Dr. John Green discovered in 1976 soon after he was hired as Miami's executive vice president in charge of finance.

Green, who came from the University of Georgia, was asked to straighten out a financial mess in athletics. And he quickly had a feeling a coaching change was needed. He became convinced while sitting in the stands at the Hurricanes' 19-10 loss late that season to Florida in Orlando's Tangerine Bowl.

"The fans around me were correctly calling the plays before Miami ran them," Green said. "It was terrible."

A week later, just before the final game at Houston, Carl Selmer's contract as head coach was terminated after two years on the job. And that began the nationwide search that ended in the hiring of Lou Saban.

Green proved to be a mover and shaker in the athletic department, and he was known as a guy who had the strongest handshake anyone had ever felt. It literally pulled people off the ground.

UM officials wanted to tell Selmer of his termination after the Houston game. But a Miami television station broke the news on Friday night before the game. So Green tracked down Selmer at a pro hockey game in Houston, where the coach had gone with his team, and told him his services would no longer be needed after the game. It was the first time a Hurricane head football coach had been fired.

TELL IT LIKE IT IS

Lou Saban had taken on so many recycling jobs he had the nickname "The Garbage Man." When he became the Hurricanes' coach in 1977, he was 55 and had coached at Washington, Northwestern, Western Illinois, and Maryland, and in the pros with Boston, Buffalo twice and Denver. He also had been athletic director at the University of Cincinnati for only 19 days.

Saban jolted his Miami players and fans by his frankness. At halftime of his first spring game, he grabbed the public address microphone and said, "We were a little sloppy in the first half. But you don't have to tell me about it. We know we have a lot of work to do, but somehow we're going to get it done."

At practice one day, as a receiver zigged when he should have zagged, Saban yelled: "Run straight like an arrow and not like a bow! Did you ever hear of Robin Hood? If he shot like that, we'd all be dead!"

At a foundation dinner he told the crowd, "There's no sense kidding you. I'm not going to tell you we've got a great future this fall, because I don't know. There are no miracles we can promise you."

That summer he underwent double coronary bypass surgery.

Bill Trout, a former UM lineman and offensive assistant under Saban and Schnellenberger, said, "I felt like a Fuller Brush salesman. Lou had had the heart operation, and he had left a few other teams, so the questions I'd get from kids' parents were just brutal: 'Is Miami going to continue football? Is Saban going to stay around a while? Is Saban going to LIVE?'"

Saban resigned after two seasons to become head coach at Army.

"Some people like to rebuild cars, I like to rebuild football programs," he said. "I thought I had done all I could do at Miami."

Lou Saban

HALFTIME HIJINKS

W hat turned out to be Saban's final game at Miami was at Gainesville and the Gators dominated the first half. For a while it seemed as if the Hurricanes weren't going to come out of the locker room for the second half, not because they didn't want to, but because Saban wasn't going to let them.

"It was Doug Dickey's last team at Florida, and the Gators came out in all blue," recalled assistant coach Bill Trout. "The seniors wanted it. Neither team was very good, and they were beating us 21-0 at the half and Lou was livid. We had future first-round draft picks Don Smith and Ottis Anderson on the team. We went in the locker room and Lou was talking to his assistants and he told Ed Cavanaugh to get the Greyhound busses ready. He said, 'I ain't going to be embarrassed, we're leaving right now.' Ed points out that the game is on ABC. Lou said, 'I don't give a damn, I am not coaching a bunch of cowards.'"

Cavanaugh talked Saban out of it. But there's more to the story, courtesy of assistant coach Billy Proulx:

"We expected to win the game, but we had a sluggish first half," Proulx said. "Florida didn't have air conditioning in the locker room for the visiting team, and that really upset some people. Jerry Anderson had been a two-time captain at Florida and he was on our staff then, primarily as the strength coach. He was so upset he decided to take it upon himself as we got ready to start the second half. The players had to walk by a coaches locker room as they went down a hallway to the field. Lou was in the doorway of the locker room and yelling at kids to play better. Jerry went berserk and took it like he was still playing. He pushed Lou aside and went right after the first kid, Don Smith, our All-America defensive tackle, and picked him up against the wall and hit him hard. Then he threw Don behind him and started grabbing other kids and whomped them on the head. In the midst of this, Jerry elbowed Lou and Lou rolled across floor and did a backward somersault and banged into the lockers. His glasses fell off and his hat was askew. Then Lou broke out in a big smile."

Trout recalled that Saban said, "It's about time someone hit somebody on this team."

Added Proulx: "The kids got so juiced that it really worked, and they went out in the second half and won the game 22-21. Ed Cavanaugh was a perfect foil. He had been with Lou before. He brought some sanity to it. But it left Jerry Anderson still insane."

MAN OF ALL SEASONS

Lou Saban was not a tunnel-vision football coach, as long-time assistant coach Billy Proulx could attest.

"When Lou first got there and had a house in the south part of the county, his daughter and son were living with him," Proulx said. "They didn't have a phone yet, and if something happened in recruiting he had to know right away. So I drove to his house and knocked on the door. His daughter answered and said, 'Come in. He's in here.' I walked in and he was in the living room in a bathrobe and pajamas, bare feet, with classical music in the background and he was playing the cello."

Proulx recalled another time when he had to get a message to Saban in the middle of practice.

"We had two practice fields, one for the offense and one for the defense," Proulx said. "Lou sometimes would work the middle. I had a message I thought was really important and I came down onto the practice field. He was doing his thing between the two fields and was talking with a couple of guys. My message was not so important as to interrupt his conversation, so I edged to try to get closer so he'd see that I had something to tell him. I could hear them talking and the dialogue was in Chinese. I didn't know until then that he interpreted Mandarin Chinese. To see my boss speak to these Orientals in Chinese, I was shocked. Lou was an old-school player who had played without a face mask. But he played the cello and spoke Chinese. He was a great man."

JET LAG KIDS

The 1979 team, Howard Schnellenberger's first, became known as the Jet Lag Kids as they traveled 28,000 miles, more than any team in the history of college football. By comparison, that season Florida traveled 6,850 miles and Florida State 5,564. The unofficial record had been 21,000 miles logged by Grambling in 1976.

The Hurricanes played seven of 11 games on the road, visiting Tallahassee twice to face FSU and Florida A&M, plus San Diego State, Buffalo to play Syracuse (while the Carrier Dome was being built), Penn State, Alabama, and Tokyo to play Notre Dame in the Mirage Bowl.

The season's theme: "Join the Hurricanes and See the World."

They traveled 7,000 miles to play a "home" game against Notre Dame that had been scheduled for the Orange Bowl. The idea began at Notre Dame, which had been coveted by promoters of the Mirage Bowl, which featured American college football teams. Football was only about a dozen years old in Japan and there were no pro teams and just a few high school teams playing the sport. But the Japanese were intrigued by the game and its pagentry and bands. In fact, the Miami and Notre Dame bands received equal billing with the football teams throughout the week as they made numerous appearances at parades and concerts.

Notre Dame didn't want to move one of it home games but considered seeking a switch with Navy, which the Irish played at neutral sites every other year, or with Miami, which drew poor crowds at the Orange Bowl.

When the offer to move the game was made in 1978,

Saban was intrigued by the idea, because it would be a recruiting tool, it would earn national publicity, and it would generate more revenue than a game in the Orange Bowl. Mirage Bowl sponsors picked up Miami's $75,000 travel expenses and guaranteed each team $200,000.

The game came right after the Hurricanes lost at top-ranked Alabama 30-0. On Tuesday before the Mirage Bowl, 55 players, 200 band members and 71 members of the official party boarded a Japan Air Lines 747 at 5:45 a.m. at Miami International Airport. Moments later they all exited because the plane had a flat tire. After an eight-hour flight and a bumpy descent, the plane stopped to refuel at Anchorage, Alaska, where Schnellenberger ordered his team to walk a mile and a half through the terminal to avoid cramping.

The Anchorage-to-Tokyo leg lasted another eight hours, then it took three hours to get through customs and to the hotel. It was Wednesday afternoon in Tokyo, the weather was drizzly and 40 degrees, and the practice field had no grass and resembled a giant mud pie.

"It looked like a reclaimed rice paddy," Schnellenberger said.

The game drew 62,674 to the Olympic Stadium and Notre Dame beat the turnover-prone Hurricanes, 40-15. At the airport after the game, UM radio announcer Ron Harrison joked that the Tokyo airport security guards were wasting their time searching the team for terrorists. "Obviously they didn't see the Notre Dame game," he said.

During the trip back, his football network sidekick Jim Gallagher penned "An Ode to the Hurricanes":

We played in the land of the rising sun, and the sun never rose.

We played against Syracuse in Buffalo, and nearly froze.
We played twice in Tallahassee. Why? Nobody knows.
When you're the Miami Hurricanes, that's the way it goes.

No Sightseeing Tour

The trip to Tokyo, in fact the entire season, was anything but a sightseeing tour.

"I thought we were going to die in Alaska when we were landing," center Don Bailey said of the 747's descent through turbulent air into Anchorage. "When we got to the hotel in Tokyo, I was on the elevator with [wide receiver] Larry Brodsky and [linebacker] Danny Brown and [guards] Art Kehoe and Clem Barbarino. Three or four Notre Dame offensive linemen got on and asked if we were in the Miami band, we were so undersized.

"[Defensive lineman] Tony Chickillo and [guard] Jim Burt missed the bus to the game and had to take a cab. We dressed at the hotel, and they were in a cab in their uniforms and walking around the stadium lost.

"Then they lined the field with lime and everybody got scarred because it burns you. All the sightseeing was from the hotel to the practice field. Howard wasn't big on that.

"And I remember in the game at Alabama, most of the team was just happy to see Bear Bryant. Nobody was really recruited by Bear. They were ranked number one and were on a roll. George Lindsey and Goober from the TV show *Mayberry* were on the sideline and we wondered if we could get an autograph after the game. We were the country boys coming to big-time football."

After the Tokyo trip, there were media reports out of Japan that several items were missing from the hotel where the teams stayed. Kehoe recalled that "our kids brought back pillows, blankets and bathrobes. During practice Howard sent two graduate assistants to our rooms and they came back with a truckload of stuff and sent it back to them in Japan.

"A story came over the wire about some jewelry being stolen. My dad called me and said, 'That wasn't you, wasn't it?' 'I said, 'Give me a little credit.'"

AND THE BANDS PLAYED ON

Jim Gallagher, who also announced UM replay telecasts in the early 1980s, recalled that when the Hurricanes' travel party arrived in Tokyo, "there was a reception table set up in the lobby. Two ladies were sitting there and they had the Mirage Bowl credentials to issue. Ron and I walked up and said, 'We're from Miami, and we're the radio team and need credentials.' They smiled and didn't say anything, and we thought, 'Oh oh, they don't speak English. We'll find somebody who does. Ron saw a Japanese-looking guy wearing a Mirage Bowl blazer and Ron said, 'I'll bet he speaks English.' He held up a University of Miami football guide with our pictures in it and pointed to it and said, 'Miami, Ron, Jim,' and shows him our pictures. 'Radio. We do radio.' The guy replies in perfect English, 'Cool it, man. I'm with the agency in Philadelphia. I went to Temple.'"

Gallagher added: "Everyone says the first thing you've got to do when you get to Tokyo is go to bed. A few minutes after we've gone to bed, there's a knock on our door. Scott Atwell or someone from the Miami sports information staff asked if we wanted the team stats. A half hour later a kid from Notre Dame knocked on the door and said, 'I've got the stats.' A half hour later, athletic director Harry Mallios called and said, 'There's a little reception. Come down to the room.' Ron said, 'Why didn't they just room us in the lobby?'"

Gallagher also recalled that before the game, the bands from both schools played the Japanese national anthem and the United States national anthem, then the University of Miami band played the Miami alma mater, and the Notre Dame band played the famed Notre Dame fight song.

"Eighty-four thousand Japanese were there and probably very few of them knew of South Bend or Miami," Gallagher said, "but they really tuned into the music. They stood up for all of the songs, including the Miami alma mater and the Notre

Dame fight song. Then during the game, every first down Notre Dame got, they played that song, and the Japanese fans stood up every time they played it. It gave new meaning to Notre Dame being not only a national team but a world team."

NEITHER SLEET NOR SNOW...

Growing up in the hilly area of western Pennsylvania and eastern Ohio known as the "Cradle of Quarterbacks," Jim Kelly envisioned following in the footsteps of Johnny Unitas, Joe Namath and Joe Montana. He also dreamed of playing in front of the 80,000 fans who jam Beaver Stadium at Penn State. But the Nittany Lions of Joe Paterno already had recruited two quarterbacks from Pennsylvania and the school that was known as Linebacker U was interested in Kelly as a linebacker. But he turned down Paterno because he wanted to play quarterback and "go to a school that throws."

Pittsburgh, Tennessee, Kentucky, Notre Dame and Miami also were interested in Kelly. And his grandfather, Pat McGinn, who emigrated from Ireland, wanted one of his grandsons to quarterback the Fighting Irish.

Lou Saban and assistant Ron Marciniak flew up on a recruiting visit during a blizzard. But the flight couldn't land in Pittsburgh and was detoured to Toronto, where they sat for six hours before returning to Pittsburgh. The roads to East Brady were snowbound. Marciniak, who had grown up near Pittsburgh, drove the rental car and kept asking Saban if he wanted to turn back.

"Just keep it on the road," Saban said.

Snow made it impossible to read the numbers on the houses, and all the houses in East Brady, as in all the old mining towns in the area, looked alike. They got out of the car and began knocking on the door of each house.

Kelly's mother was delayed in getting home because of the

storm. So when Saban arrived at the Kelly household, he yanked off his tie, stuck a towel in the front of his belt and began to make dinner. He also pointed out there wouldn't be any blizzards in Miami. Instead, there would be a lot of sparkling water and a lot of pretty women. And Kelly would be quarterbacking a pro-style offense.

Saban pulled out a pencil and paper and drew pass patterns, showing how zone defenses rotated, etc. Kelly was impressed, especially because of Saban's experience as a pro coach with Denver and Buffalo.

Saban admitted the program was on shaky ground financially, and Kelly knew it would be risky to go there. But once he visited the campus, on his first trip to Florida, he knew Miami was the perfect place for him. He visited in November, went to the beaches and saw the coeds in bikinis, and went to some discos. "I saw more beautiful women and said, 'Where do I sign?'"

SEEING GREATNESS

Former athletic director Dr. Harry Mallios recalls one day in 1978 looking out the window of his office and seeing Lou Saban down on the practice field looking down in the dumps. So Mallios went down to cheer him up.

"How are things going?" Mallios said.

"Oh, I don't know, Harry," Saban replied. "I'm trying to put this together."

Saban was watching the quarterbacks go through drills and said, "I don't think he's gonna do it for us. Or him. But see that kid? He's going to be the one to turn it around."

The player? Jim Kelly.

IN THE LIONS' DEN

In addition to the upset victory at Auburn in 1978, the game that signalled the Hurricanes were turning their program around came late in the 1979 season at Penn State. Behind the passing of surprise first-time starter Jim Kelly, they built a 10-0 lead before the 19th-ranked Nittany Lions ran an offensive play.

"We didn't know Kelly would start," said Art Kehoe, who played guard in that game. "We'd practiced all week with Kelly and Mike Rodriguez. I was jacked up. I traded with teammates for 30 tickets for my mom and dad and four sisters and my brother and his wife and 10 or 12 friends who had driven up from my home town of Conshohocken, Pennsylvania.

"The night before the game my buddies, who attended Penn State, knocked on the door at our hotel. John Canine, an offensive lineman, was my roommate. He opened the door and I was snoring away and the my friends jumped on me. They were drunk and Canine threw them out. They were yelling, 'Bruce Clark and Matt Millan are going to kick your tail.'

"At breakfast I was reading the local paper and they said the Nittany Lions were favored by 40 points. When we left breakfast, John and I walked back to our room. We walked past Kelly's room and all of East Brady was there. They were all screaming, 'Good luck.' Howard walked by with his pipe and he stuck his head in the door and growled, 'What the hell is going on? I came to tell you you'd be the starting quarterback but now I don't know if I should.' His friends scattered like rats.

"Before every game, Kelly would puke. But in this one it was a landslide of vomit, all over the grass field. He wiped his hands and went in the huddle and called a play and handed off to Chris Hobbs, who went 50 yards.

"Another thing that stood out was all the green and orange in the stands behind the Penn State bench. It was a dreary day and Penn State was wearing their boring blue and white. When the game was over we flew across the field and over their bench and celebrated with the fans. We had so many players from

Western Pennsylvania, Ohio and New York.

"After our first touchdown we kicked a high pooch kick that got caught in the wind, and Mike Godeker caught it in the air. It was amazing.

"After the game Schnellenberger sent his entire staff throughout the state on a rampage to recruit. Everywhere they stopped they'd say, 'Anybody know the score of last week's game?'"

Kehoe on Kelly barf: "That was just a constant every game. We grew to expect it that Jim was going to throw up. That meant that Jim was ready to play and that kind of got us all ready to play.

"I remember the night before hearing the predicted score was 30-0. It seemed like everybody was just into the game and not even worrying about the score. We were playing with abandon. We were loose and played well."

CHAPTER 4

Character and Characters

A PIPE DREAM?

Don Mariutto Sr. was on Miami's board of trustees at that time when the athletic department was struggling and the football coach's office was like a revolving door. That didn't faze Howard Schnellenberger, who left his position of offensive coordinator of the Miami Dolphins to try to help resurrect the Hurricanes' program.

"We'd gotten rid of basketball [in 1971] and some board members wanted to do away with football and intercollegiate athletics," Mariutto said. "We had to struggle to stay alive. John Green was hired as executive vice president and he saw that we got funded. If it weren't for him, I'm not sure we would have made it.

"I remember a meeting with Howard Schnellenberger soon after he was hired in 1979, and he discussed his plans for a stadium on campus. He showed us a composite drawing in the first yearbook of a planned stadium on campus. He said, 'We're going to win the national championship.'

"I thought it was so absurd I could hardly believe it. We could hardly keep a coach, and to have one with his stature was amazing. I thought this guy was dreaming. It was hard to keep a straight face. I said, 'Well, Coach, you have my support. Just win a few games.'"

BUILDING TRADITION

B illy Proulx, who had been with the program as an assistant coach for several years, remembers Schnellenberger's sense of history and of building tradition soon after he replaced Saban in December of 1978.

"Howard did something for those seniors who had gone 2-8, 3-8, 3-8 and 6-5," Proulx said. "They had played for Lou. We had a banquet at a restaurant, and Howard decided to do something for those seniors like Ottis Anderson and Ken Johnson and Don Smith. He said, 'You were here when it was only the beginning.' He treated those kids like they were his, and he made them feel real good about their experience and what they helped us do. I'd worked for four head coaches, and this was the first time I'd seen any of our coaches bridge from one coach to another. He wasn't ignoring what happened before and acting as if he would be the only person to create history. He invited Lou to come down for the banquet. I guess Lou couldn't because of spring practice at Army, but Lou agreed to videotape something to each of those kids. Howard gave the spotlight to Saban to talk to those kids.

"It was a wonderful thing to do. It showed the kind of guy Saban was even after he left and what Howard was going to be. Howard loves tradition and loves to set it, but he respects what happened. Those were the first kids who felt they could come back and they won't be forgotten. When spring practice began they came around."

THE STATE OF MIAMI

Lou Saban believed the two most important ways to turn the program around were recruiting and putting fans in the Orange Bowl. He succeeded at recruiting as he and his staff went on an unprecedented recruiting blitz in Florida, especially from Miami to Palm Beach County. The Hurricanes usually had lost the top recruits in South Florida to the Oklahomas, Ohio States and Notre Dames.

That changed forever with Saban's recruiting class of 1978. Nineteen of the 30 signees were from Florida, the most ever from the state to that time. Six were first-team All-State selections, including Lester Williams, the nation's premier lineman; Larry Brodsky, David Jefferson, Mark Richt, Chris Duffy and Mike Rodrigue. The class also included Jim Kelly from Pennsylvania.

Howard Schnellenberger took that a step further by creating what he called "The State of Miami," which was everything south of Orlando. At times during the recruiting season, Schnellenberger would walk into the coaches' meeting room and stare for an hour at the large orange and green lists on the wall that ranked dozens of prospects.

"He wouldn't say a thing," recalled Suzy Wilkoff, Miami's recruiting coordinator from 1981-83. "It was like these guys were going to sign just by wishing it."

In the spring of 1982, at the top of his wish list was signing two of the best high school quarterbacks in the nation. It came true when Miami landed the quarterbacks they rated No. 1 and No. 3 in the nation, Bernie Kosar and Vinny Testaverde.

THE EASTER SEALS RUN

In the spring of 1980, Schnellenberger and promotions director Roy Hamlin came up with an idea to bring the team together, create interest in the football program and help a char-ity—a 221-mile run with a football from the Cape Kennedy Space Center to Miami Beach to benefit Easter Seals.

"The plan was to run the team in two-mile increments from Cape Kennedy to the Fontainebleau Hotel and get expo-sure for the team, bring Miami football to them. Billy Proulx and I went up and got vans and all the coaches were involved. We started at Cape Kennedy with the directors and the upcom-ing astronauts. Howard and Jim Burt and Jim Kelly and maybe Mark Rush started the first leg. They'd run a mile and the van would be there to pick them up and have a fresh group of play-ers take over. And the idea was to not drop the ball, and they never did.

"We came down with the van around the fourth or fifth leg and nobody showed up. A building under construction had collapsed, and they had to detour around it. Howard and Kelly and Rush and Burt were running, and they ended up running around eight miles instead of two.

"Overall the event really was successful. Don Bailey's dad helped with housing overnight near Vero Beach. It took a lot of coordination, and it brought coaches together and the players together. Nobody slacked off. It took two days. People would run with us and pledge so much money a mile. We raised sever-al thousands of dollars for Easter Seals."

Ed Hudak, a reserve defensive lineman on that team and now a security liaison for the team, remembered the Easter Seals Run as "A typical sales job by the head coach. He told us we'd have to run maybe a half-mile but each of us ran 10 miles. The first thing we got when we left Cape Kennedy was a flat tire on 826. Were not even out of Dade County. We got to Vero Beach during the run and coach Bill Trout pulled the van over to into the sugar sand and we got stuck."

TALE OF THE TAPE

Imagine Bobby Bowden and Howard Schnellenberger putting on boxing gloves, stepping into the ring and shadow boxing to pump up interest in their game. It happened in 1980.

When Miami and Florida State meet now, obviously no hype is needed. For more than three decades they have had one of the premier rivalries in the nation. But that wasn't the case in 1980 when the Seminoles were just starting to take off under Bowden and the Hurricanes were still trying to establish themselves under Schnellenberger.

The teams met in the fourth game of the season at the Orange Bowl. Early the week of the game, Schnellenberger flew to Tallahassee and staged a "photo op" with Bowden, complete with boxing gloves, a tale of the tape and, of course, Howard's pipe. No punches were landed.

The coaches also played cards for the cameras. "It can now be revealed," said Roy Hamlin, "that Howard had the cards stacked so he would win."

The game attracted 50,008, double the attendance at the 1978 game in the Orange Bowl and the largest home crowd in 11 years. The unranked Hurricanes beat ninth-rated FSU 10-9.

NO SWEAT IN GAINESVILLE

In July of 1980, Schnellenberger and Proulx flew to Gainesville to scout accommodations for the Florida game. Proulx's recollection of the trip gives insight into the forceful, demanding, never-miss-a-detail approach by Schnellenberger.

"At one motel," Proulx said, "he was so demanding about every little facility that I couldn't believe it. Here it was midsummer and I was wearing a polo shirt and he had on a wool three-piece suit and he was telling off the manager. And Howard wasn't even sweating. He wasn't sweating because he simply refused to sweat."

Schnellenberger made a deal with the motel, but there was no restaurant there, so he and Proulx sought a place for the team to eat on Friday night and Saturday morning. They went to a posh country club, where the manager said they had never had a football team eat there.

"That settled it for Howard," said Proulx. "We made the deal. Then, on our way out, he turned to me and said, 'Can you imagine what this place will be like when we come in here 10-0?' We didn't make it, [they came in 7-3] but that's when it really sank in to me what kind of man he is. He has a lot of Bear Bryant in him."

RETALIATION AT FLORIDA

In that final regular-season game in 1980 at Florida, the unranked Hurricanes upset the 18th-ranked Gators 31-7. Gator fans were nasty, pelting the UM bench throughout the game with oranges, tangerines, ice, rolls of toilet paper (unused), water cups, etc.

Schnellenberger was so furious that he called for a 35-yard field goal attempt after UM recovered a fumble in the last second of the game. Danny Miller's kick was good, but it never showed up on the scoreboard, which was turned off immediately after the game ended.

"The field goal was my little way of telling the fans I was not happy with their conduct," Schnellenberger said.

Florida players and coaches were insulted and vowed to get revenge the next season. Al Michaels, who called the game for ABC, closed by saying, "Wouldn't that stick in Florida's craw somewhere down the line?"

Thinking Peach

Instead of bowls wooing the Miami Hurricanes, the roles were reversed in 1980. The Canes hadn't played in a bowl game in 14 years, and they practically had to jump up and down and shout to get the attention of bowl officials.

On the first day bowl invitations could be extended, Miami defeated Vanderbilt 24-17 to improve its record to 6-3. But no bowls came calling. In fact, a 5-4 Houston team that lost to the Hurricanes 14-7 received a bid.

Late that night, Schnellenberger learned that North Carolina backed out of its commitment to play in the Peach Bowl in Atlanta. The coach was determined to get his foot in the door.

He called longtime friend Charley Thornton, who was assistant athletic director at Alabama and who had been Miami's athletic director briefly in 1980.

"How do I arouse interest in the Peach Bowl?" Schnellenberger asked.

"Call them," Thornton said.

Schnellenberger reached a Peach Bowl official and said, "You're about to make a terrible mistake. We may have one of the best teams in the country, and we're not even on your list."

Peach Bowl officials suddenly said Miami was on their list "as an afterthought." Prime candidates remained Stanford, Indiana, Louisiana State and Kansas.

The following Monday, UM officials stepped up their blitz for the Peach Bowl. Athletic director Dr. Harry Mallios and administrative assistant Billy Proulx flew to Atlanta and pointed out that Miami's record was better than other Peach Bowl contenders and better than many schools playing in the postseason. They also pointed out the Hurricanes played a schedule ranked the second toughest in the nation, and they promised to sell 10,000 tickets.

Schnellenberger then took his campaign to South Florida, beseeching fans to attend that week's game in the Orange Bowl against North Texas State.

"I'm hollering for help," he said as he sat behind four cans of peaches. "This is the most important week the football department has had in a long time."

The response was so-so. Businessmen bought $5,000 worth of tickets to give to youth groups for the North Texas State game and cans of peaches were handed out to fans; alumnus Emerson Allsworth sent a check for $5,000 to the Peach Bowl for tickets if Miami received a bid, and alumni rented a plane to fly over downtown Atlanta carrying a sign reading: "UM ALUMNI THINKING PEACH BOWL."

Schnellenberger also instructed Ron Stone, head of the school's Young Alumni Association, to make sure Peach Bowl officials received VIP treatment when coming to Miami for the North Texas State game. Stone made sure the airline tickets for the Peach Bowl officials were upgraded to first class, and he met them at the Miami Airport. As they drove out of the airport, a large electric sign read: "WELCOME PEACH BOWL COMMITTEE. WE WANT IT!"

The officials were quartered in a hotel VIP suite, served lobster at dinner and received Hurricane jerseys with their names sewn on. Even members of the Orange Bowl Committee lobbied the Peach Bowl on behalf of the Hurricanes.

An underwhelming 20,293 showed up for the North Texas State game, but the Hurricanes' 26-8 victory apparently impressed the Peach Bowl. Or maybe the lobster did. Or maybe it was because Stanford, Indiana and Kansas lost and LSU withdrew its name because of a rash of injuries.

In any case, an hour after the game Peach Bowl selection committee chairman Art Gregory entered the Hurricanes' locker room and said, "On behalf of the Peach Bowl, I extend an invitation to ..." No one could hear the rest through the players' shouts of, "Peach! Peach! Peach!"

Schnellenberger was asked if peaches would be served more often at the training table. "We always serve peaches at our pregame meal," he said. "They're a fine source of extra sugar." He added, "Thank God we didn't get invited to the Gator Bowl."

IT'S MILLER TIME

Danny Miller not only put the finishing touches on the 1980 victory at Gainesville but made sure the Gators didn't get revenge the next season at the Orange Bowl. He has vivid memories of both games.

"At Gainesville our team had pretty much dominated that game and was thoroughly in control of everything that happened on the field," Miller said. "We weren't in control of what was happening in the stands. With us recovering a fumble with one second left, Coach Schnellenberger took the opportunity to exert a little influence over the stands and kick a field goal and maybe punish the hometown fans a little more."

And what did Schnellenberger say to him before the kick?

"Just get out there and kick it," Miller recalled. "I wasn't paying attention and wasn't ready to go out there. I just ran out there at the spur of the moment and kicked it. I didn't have time to think about it."

In the opening game of the 1981 at the Orange Bowl, Jim Kelly suffered a calf injury late in the third quarter and left the game. Mark Richt replaced him and rescued the Hurricanes from a 20-11 deficit.

"We were behind a good bit of the game and got big touchdowns by Mark Richt to Rocky Belk and Glenn Dennison to bring us back," said Miller. "We ended up with fourth and long at the 38-yard line and we were behind 20-18. Coach called a timeout and was getting ready to send in another play. I thought, 'Fourth and long or me kicking a 55-yard field goal.' I kicked that far in practice and knew I could kick it that far, so I told him, 'I can make it.' So he said, 'Well, get in there and make it.' And the rest is history.

"I hit it well. I knew I pulled it a little bit left. You can always tell, like a golf shot. You can feel the way you hit it. I knew it was going to be a little bit close. I didn't know it hit the upright until it was all over. I had no idea at the time."

A film of the play shot for Miami television station WTVJ was from a lower angle and showed the ball actually hitting the crossbar, then the upright and going through for a 21-20 victory.

DRIVEN BY CHARACTERS

Art Kehoe has been involved in Hurricanes football longer than anyone currently in the program. An offensive guard on the 1979 and 1980 teams, he has been on the coaching staff all but five seasons (2006-2010) since 1981. He has been to 19 bowl games with the Hurricanes and has worked with six head coaches. Could anybody else be Mr. Hurricanes Football?

"When I came here in '79, I got into what is the finest program in the history of the game," said Kehoe. "To me, Miami football always has been about character and characters. To be a Hurricane you've got to have character, and part of being the Canes is being a character.

"We are so spoiled with winning, we remember the losses more. What drives you is the characters.

"A lot of the players who have come through here are real factors in society. They're good dads, good workers, they're committed, tough, and successful in life. When I think of that 1980 Peach Bowl team hanging around in my house, all I think of is characters and character.

"No matter what I do in my lifetime, the guys who were part of that team and a little after all know the school has gone on to bigger and better things. We triggered it. There's a lot of pride. Coach Schnellberger probably ran off 20 to 25 guys, so the guys who survived were mentally tough and committed to each other. Battle tested and tried."

Art Kehoe

THE ROOMMATES

Perhaps the epitome of a dorm room filled with characters and character was the one that contained Kehoe and defensive linemen Jim Burt and Tony Fitzpatrick. The fourth roommate "always had a problem and moved out," said Kehoe. "We kept a clean room. The coaches liked to check our room because we were a bunch of characters, they knew some storytelling would be going on.

"Burt would bring a 16-millimeter projector and we'd watch film. Fitz had a different girlfriend every other week. He kept us in stitches.

"I remember the time he took Burt's car after curfew to sneak over to Wendy's. Jim caught him and shaved the few chest hairs he had off his chest. He had to practice the next week with big bandages, and his chest broke out in hives. Jim would sneak into the shower and tear the bandages off.

"We were there two years, in room 36R. Guys were always coming by our place and playing backgammon."

Jim Kelly says Burt, who went on to become one of the NFL's best nose tackles with the New York Giants and whose son was a star on the Hurricanes' baseball team, liked pulling pranks on everybody. Burt was known as a guy who had to get in the last word on every conversation and was called "One-Up," because no matter what anybody said, he always had to go one better.

MIDNIGHT PEP RALLY

Kehoe recalled that "one of best stories was in 1980 when we beat Florida State with Burt blocking a two-point conversion to win 10-9. FSU had a 26-game unbeaten streak and we were 4-0. There were 80,000 people in the Orange Bowl, half Noles and half Canes.

"On Tuesday, Wednesday and Thursday we had big practices. Thursday night before the game, right after bed check,

Jim Kelly (12) and Jim Burt (83)

Burt wakes me and Fitz up at 12:30 in the morning. I said, 'What's up?' Burt said, 'Just shut up and get outside.' He went upstairs and got Jim Joiner, Pat Walker, Jim Pokorney, Mark Smith, Mozell Axon, and Scott Nicolas out of bed in their underwear. We went out back behind Building 36 and did jumping jacks and spelled out Miami. Everybody is screaming and yelling. Then the dorms next to us woke up and everybody came out, and the next thing you know we're starting a pep rally and bonfire.

"The police came and knew we were having fun and parked around us and turned on their lights and we had a rally until 1:30 in morning. I remember going to bed and thinking, 'I know this week we've worked our tails off and we've got a team that cares about each other and we're going to lay it on the line against FSU.'

"I remember when we came out on the field, the public address announcer Jay Rokeach said, 'Welcome to Miami's

Orange Bowl. It's 12 noon and the temperature is 92 and the relative humidity is 93 percent. Have a nice day.'

"It was a typical FSU bloodletting. Burt dominated the second- and third-team centers, and that was the difference in the game. I remember after the game we were so exhausted we could barely go out and party.

"That game set a standard that we were tough and together."

THE BREAKFAST CLUB

If players didn't follow Howard Schnellenberger's strict regimen, they faced the consequences: The Breakfast Club. And it wasn't to chow down on pancakes and bacon.

"Coach told us that every day of our lives there will be bed check, breakfast check, lunch check, dinner check, classroom check. You're going to do that stuff or run in the morning. There were never girls in dorm and barely families.

"Fitz and Burt and I had to go to the Breakfast Club. Assistant coach Harold Allen had us rolling the whole field, puking all over place and getting dizzy. That's all I remember."

Fitzpatrick remembered more. "Jim and I would eat a breakfast of a big omelette, bacon and sausage and go back to bed. Then we'd get up at 11 and lift weights. My GPA didn't go up too high.

"Coach Harold Allen, who made a man out of me, found out what we were doing and took us to the Breakfast Club at 6 a.m. and we'd crawl 100 yards, carry each other's legs, and run three and a half miles every day for two and a half weeks. Jim was the biggest actor and made it look like he was in a coma."

MORE ROOMMATES TALES

Tony Fitzpatrick was typical of many "reclamation projects" that Schnellenberger and his staff pulled off in building Miami's first national championship team. He had no scholarship out of high school in St. Petersburg, Florida, but by his senior season in 1983, Schnellenberger was calling this middle guard "the rock of our defense."

"The recruiters said I was too short," Fitzpatrick said. "I took the best thing I could and signed with Liberty University, where Sam Rutigliano was the head coach. I played in the state high school all-star game and Howard saw me in the game. Everybody else at the game had a scholarship. I had 15 tackles and got the MVP award for the South team, and Howard came down to the field and said, 'I want to give you a scholarship if we have one.'

"After two days at Liberty, Miami called and said I got a scholarship. There were no rooms left and just one bed left in the room with Jim Burt, Art Kehoe and Jeff Salinger, who smoked cigarettes and was a senior. I said, 'I can't handle this [smoking],' and I kicked him out of the room, but he didn't cause a problem. I thought it was great. Then Jim and Art drew straws, and the next thing I knew all my things were in Art's room. Jim made his room into a palace. We'd shoot skyrockets out of his dorm room, we'd order moving vans to his room, five or six pizzas at a time.

"Jim and Art also had a roulette wheel and had a gambling casino going on in their room. One day there was a knock at the door, and it was the campus police. I dove out the back window and ran to my girlfriend's house, and they almost got arrested.

"Jim trained with Harold Ross, the world-class kick boxer. Art and I would go to his room and he'd make us put our bottoms up against the wall, and we'd take all the furniture out, and he made us go almost into a full stretch. It kept us so flexible."

Tony Fitzpatrick

PLAYING FOR HOWARD

Fitzpatrick, who became a radio announcer in Houston, mirrored the rags-to-riches story of the Hurricanes under Howard Schnellenberger. He arrived at Miami in

Schnellenberger's first season, and by the end of his senior season the Canes had pulled off the "Miracle of Miami" and stunned Nebraska for the national title.

"Before Howard got there, Miami was a vacation spot for coaches," Fitzpatrick said. "They'd go there for two years and get a good tan and leave. Coach Schnellenberger made a commitment and said, 'I'll give you a national championship in five years.' If there had been a 50-story building, he'd make you believe you could walk up the side of it. Whether it was the weight room, classes, you took it to the bank. He came from the NFL, won a Super Bowl with the undefeated 1972 Miami Dolphins as offensive coordinator, and coached the Baltimore Colts. We took everything he said to heart. He made a man out of a lot of guys who came from different backgrounds—kids from broken homes, no dads.

"We had guys like Don Bailey and Danny Brown and Kevin Fagan and Fred Robinson and Jay Brophy, Ken Sisk, Jack Fernandez, Ken Calhoun. And the offensive line was the ultimate international line—an Italian, a Cuban, an African-American and a Canadian who looked like an albino and a white guy who looked like he played in a rock band.

"We loved each other. What we went through in practice—we beat the dog snot out of each other Tuesday through Thursday. Saturday was easy, those guys had to pay. Ray Ganong, the strength coach, made a man out of a lot of them. He put you through a routine where your muscles were screaming. After the first year we were there, Florida State knew the difference when we stepped on field next year.

"After going 5-6 the first season, the next year we lost a lot of games in the fourth quarter. The next spring we went through the off season where we had to go to eight stations for 40 minutes, and we were all throwing up. It was unbelievable. After that we'd do 10 100s. If somebody would drop, they'd stop the 100s, the trainers would tote them off the field and we'd start again.

"When somebody went down during practice, Howard would turn the practice around [away from the injured players]

and keep going. I blew my knee out, Leon Evans hyperextended his elbow, and Coach turned practice around. He made you
understand what hard work was. There was no gray area.

"People thought Jerome Brown was the first to do the
fatigues. But Darin McMurray and I went to the Orange Bowl
game against Nebraska in fatigues. My head was shaved, we
were ready for war.

"When the first snap happened, Nebraska knew they were
in a dog fight. And we shouldn't have been on the same field.
They were far superior. They had the Heisman winner, and the
Lombardi winner, and their offensive line would blow out teams
by 50 to 60 points. People still talk about that game and it's seen
on *ESPN Classic*.

"Don Bailey [the center] and I had wars in practice for
four years. After practice we'd sit next to each other and say,
'Why do we do this?' Blood's running out our noses, we'd have
scratches all over us. But to this day we're like brothers. He got
me into broadcasting."

SUNDAY MORNING SCRIMMAGE

Usually Sundays during the season are a day for players to get
rehabilitation, stretch and look at game film. Full-blown
practices are rare, especially with the current NCAA restrictions
on Division I football. Howard Schnellenberger made an exception one weekend in 1982, and former center Don Bailey
believes that may have paved the way to the first national championship a year later.

"We lost to Florida State 24-7 at homecoming on TV in a
4:00 game," recalled Bailey, who has been a color commentator
on the Hurricanes' radio network for several years. "Howard had
us in the locker room after the game. He said there would be
bed check and curfew would be 11:00. He bedchecked everybody. And the next morning at 8:00 we went through a full-

blown practice and scrimmage with the number-one offense against the number-one defense.

"Back then a lot of guys played the whole game, there was not a lot of rotation. That practice and what he did right there had as much to do in really setting the tone for what it takes to win a national championship. We didn't get out of the Orange Bowl until 8:00. By the time you'd eat and get in bed it was 11. And we were in full pads Sunday morning. Usually we'd come in for meetings at 3:30 and get treatment. There were no days off with Howard. But nobody was really surprised."

Bailey remembered that in Schnellenberger's first season, 1979, he set the standard for conditioning.

"He brought in the 12-minute run from the Dolphins," Bailey said. "It's safe to say maybe half the team didn't make it. Through training camp he had everybody do a three-and-a-half mile run at 6 or 6:30 in the morning for a time. If you did not make it, you'd have to run again on Sunday. We'd run, eat breakfast, get taped, go through the first practice, take a nap, and then come back for practice. We didn't do this once, but for days at a time. He got away with it. Nobody knew better, and everybody wanted to be there.

"That's why everybody laughs at this 20-hour [NCAA] rule now. Every night you'd come back and have meetings until 8:30 or 9. We'd do 20 hours the first two days."

THE DYSFUNCTION BOYS

More of Bailey's recollection of Schnellenberger's boot camps: "Howard relied on trainer Mike O'Shea. Mike would tell him the guys were spent, and then he pushed them again.

"It got so bad ... everybody talks about water today. We had one five-minute water break at every practice and that was it. It got to the point that if guys got injured and had bags of ice on their knee or shoulder, they'd drink the melted ice. When

Howard Schnellenberger

players got caught they would rip the ice off them or put iodine in the water so they couldn't drink it.

"Then we'd go out a half hour before practice and hide ice bags in goalpost pads or bushes, then go sneak a break and grab a little ice.

"He'd say if we had practice and somebody got hurt, just slide the drill over. Never miss a play. Bear Byant had the Junction Boys. I think Howard had the Dysfunction Boys. He took a bunch of dysfunctional players and made them into something special.

"He also knew whom to make captains. Having Art Kehoe and Jim Burt for the year we won the Peach Bowl [1980] was no accident. He realized if he could get Burt to believe in him, Jim would police everyone else. Kehoe was just a great leader in his own right."

Bailey noted that Schnellenberger had a knack of knowing when to tighten the screws in practice and when to ease off a bit. An example from the 1981 season:

"We lost to 16th-ranked Mississippi State 14-10 on the road in as physical a game as you can imagine. The fans had the cow bells, and John Bond was at quarterback. We came back from Mississippi State, and on Monday, Tuesday and Wednesday we were in full pads. And Thursday we had a live goal-line scrimmage with the ones versus the ones. And Friday we were dying and we went to East Carolina. It's cold and nasty, and the referee called a penalty and spit two false teeth on the field.

"We won 31-6 and we came back Saturday night, and we were dead. Howard had killed us. Then we came out on Monday and he put us in shorts, which never happened. We had never been without pads on a Tuesday or Wednesday, ever. So on Tuesday we went in pads and had a regular practice, and Wednesday we were in shorts and shoulder pads. Thursday we were in shorts, and Friday was regular. He went from a very tough, tough week after the loss to the easiest week we'd ever known under Howard Schnellenberger, and we went out and beat the number-one team in the country, Penn State, 17-14. It amazes me to this day how he was able to make that happen. That's coaching.

THE MORRALL OF THE STORY

When Howard Schnellenberger put his staff together in 1979, an ingenious move was the hiring of Earl Morrall to coach the quarterbacks. An All-American at Michigan State, Morrall was a quarterback in the NFL for 21 years, including his last five with the Dolphins through 1976. When starter Bob Griese was injured early in the undefeated 1972 season, Morrall filled in superbly until Griese returned for the Super Bowl.

With the Hurricanes, Morrall helped develop Jim Kelly, Mark Richt, Kyle Vanderwende, Bernie Kosar and Vinny Testaverde. Kelly said, "The best thing that ever happened" to his football career was when Schnellenberger brought in Morrall. He taught Kelly all the basics of throwing. "He didn't care whether you started or played third string, you did things his way, or you did them somewhere else," Kelly said. "He was as tough as they come."

Kelly noted that after a two-and-a-half-hour practice, players would run gassers, running back and forth across the width of the field four times. If they didn't finish each within 40 seconds, with a 30-second break in between, Morrall would make them run four or five more.

SCARED TO LAUGH

Players often wondered whether the six-foot-one, 230-pound poker-faced man with the pipe and mustache ever had a sense of humor.

"It's hard to tell when he's kidding and when he isn't," said Scott Atwell, a student assistant in the sports information office. "You're scared to laugh and you're scared not to."

Wide receiver Pat Walker added: "For a year and a half, I thought he was just a mean man, with all those rules he gave us. I thought I would never hear him tell a joke. But when he started smiling and joking around every now and then, we just didn't know he had another side."

CHAPTER 5

It's a Miracle

OFF ON THE RIGHT FOOTE

The 1981 season-opening game against Florida also marked the first game for new UM president Edward T. Foote II, who replaced the retiring Henry King Stanford. Foote was spared an embarrassing moment in front of a huge crowd of Hurricane fans thanks to longtime board of trustees member and alumni president Ron Stone.

"I put together an alumni tent for parties across the street from the east end zone," Stone said. "I told Foote and Howard Schnellenberger that they had to come to this before the game. We had 1,800 people there. The head coach shows up 15 minutes before kickoff, and Foote shows up in a blazer.

"I had a huge bread Gator and wanted them to take a bite out of it. Foote had an orange and blue tie on, he had no clue those were the Gators' colors. I told him he couldn't wear it and he said, 'Why not? My wife bought it for me.'

"John Lisk, who later became president of the alumni association, was wearing a green and white tie and he yanked it off and gave it to the president. Howard walked in and the place went crazy. Howard introduced the new president and said, 'To initiate you the right way, take a bite.' And the place went wild."

WHERE THERE'S SMOKE...

Roy Hamlin, president of an advertising agency in Fort Myers, Florida, met Howard Schnellenberger during his first season at Miami in 1979. He quickly hit it off with the promotion-minded coach and became promotions and public relations director for football. It was Hamlin who came up with the idea of Schnellenberger's pipe being sort of a trademark like the houndstooth hats were for Alabama's Paul "Bear" Bryant. Hamlin's firm produced the coach's show for Miami through all the championship seasons, and he remembered the time when the pipe nearly stole the show.

"Howard had a pipe, but he didn't smoke it on the show," Hamlin said. "He'd put it out. When he'd lift it up and light it, you'd see his Super Bowl ring. Later, after he won the national championship, he used both hands and both had rings.

"I said, 'You ought to use that pipe.' At the time there was not the big concern about smoking that there is today. It was The Pipe, like a trademark. Everybody started to know him as the man with the pipe. We even gave out pipe lapel pins. He could go into a no-smoking area and nobody would say a word.

"When we were doing the show live at channel 7, he'd bang the pipe out and put it in his pocket. One time we were in a two-minute commercial break and he lit his pipe, took a couple of puffs and put it back in his pocket. Dave Willingham was the host, and we came back from the break and I saw this smoke and saw Dave's eyes looking, and the pipe was burning right through Howard's pocket. There weren't flames, but his pocket was starting to melt, and we were on live TV. I wondered if I should bring a bucket of water and Dave said, 'We move to further action.' I was trying to point to it, and we went to a break, and we said to Willingham that Coach's coat was on fire. It was embarrassing, but Howard shook it off. He laughed about it and went back to the show. We didn't say anything, we didn't want to embarrass him. He always wanted it to be right."

THE AURA

With the pipe and guttural voice, Schnellenberger had such an aura about him that players knew he was coming into the locker room even though they couldn't see him.

"When he walked in the locker room, everybody got quiet," said receiver Eddie Brown. "Even though you didn't see

Eddie Brown

him, you knew he was coming because of the smell of that pipe."

Center Don Bailey recalled that when "I went to visit him when he was coaching in Louisville, the president and athletic director of the university were there and so were a lot of recruits. He walked in the room and everybody was talking and they took a whiff and the place went silent. The combination of the clearing of the throat and the pipe just shut it down, adults included."

TELEVISION PERSONALITIES

Here are Hamlin's recollections of working with Schnellenberger's successors on their weekly television show:

"Jimmy Johnson always wanted to look good, but he was more concerned that he said the right thing than he was about his hair or whether his tie was straight. He wanted to give a professional image.

"Dennis Erickson was a funnier guy. They all were easy to work with and had a good sense of humor. They took an interest in what you were going to do on the show. We did interviews in locker rooms, and he'd choose offensive and defensive players of the game. He was probably more interested in what the kids said.

"Butch Davis was really involved in bringing out the rest of the university, and so was Larry Coker. Every show Larry wanted an assistant coach featured, not demanding but asking, 'Is there a way to get the assistant involved and get some exposure?' We did a feature every show about what the assistant did and how he did it and we had them on the show often. And we were doing things around the university.

"Butch wanted to show the university in other academic areas. We featured some of the deans and would integrate in some of the academic stuff. He was really into bringing the team into the community, such as 'Choose A Team, Not a Gang,' show some involvement in the community, and show some of the other coaches.

"Larry Coker is probably the most humble and probably the most thankful for what you're doing. The most appreciative. He couldn't do enough for you. He never got rattled or riled up if the equipment didn't work and we had to do it again. It was kind of like working with your uncle. He was 'Larry' where everybody else was 'Coach.'

"We came over the day of the 9-11 attacks to do his show and had done the show [before the hijacked planes hit the Twin Towers]. We had to make some changes and he came right out and made the changes and changed the whole thing. It was very patriotic."

AHEAD OF THE TIMES

With Schnellenberger's penchant for public relations and Hamlin's expertise, the Hurricanes became trendsetters in television coverage of games and the coach's show.

"We also produced replays of entire games," Hamlin said. "This was prior to ESPN. The NCAA had a rule that you couldn't broadcast a game unless it was 200 miles from a competing school. We measured 203 miles to Gainesville, so we were able in the early years to broadcast our games and use cameras from Miami Dolphins TV. We'd produce the games, and we took them to the USA Network and put them on nationwide. We also were the first to uplink his coach's show. Stations would rebroadcast them in 1979 and 1980."

ON THE CAMPAIGN TRAIL

Following the Kickoff Classic meeting with Auburn at the Meadowlands in 1984, the Hurricanes played a "home" game against Florida at Tampa Stadium. As a symbolic gesture to make it Miami's home field, Schnellenberger wanted to plant his own grass seed at Tampa Stadium.

The previous May, a few weeks before Schnellenberger left for the USFL job, Hamlin put together a media trip via an Amtrak train from Miami to Tampa to drum up interest in the game and to plant the seeds.

"It was on Sam Jankovich's first day as athletic director," Hamlin said. "We picked up the media all the way along and fed them. We had a stop at Fort Lauderdale and went to Orlando and cut across the state. It was like the old days on the campaign trail, a whistle-stop thing. We had 30 people. And the train had one whole car of little kids who were taking a day trip. Howard came back to the car wearing a conductor's hat and looked like Captain Kangaroo. We planted the grass seed over there to promote the game. This was going to be our field. It probably was bluegrass from Kentucky [where Schnellenberger grew up and played college football]. Tampa thought this was cool, and we felt it was a good way to market the game."

THE HURRICANE HOWL

Another Schnellenberger/Hamlin production was the Hurricane Howl. "The Gators had the Gator Growl [a giant pep rally and entertainment extravaganza the night before the Homecoming game], and we wanted the Hurricane Howl," Hamlin recalled. "Howard said, 'I want a concert. We want music that white people will enjoy and black people will enjoy.'

"I went to the Orange Bowl and they said they weren't allowing concerts. Nevertheless, we started looking for groups that everybody would enjoy, and we got the Beach Boys and the Commodores for the same show. We went to the Orange Bowl, and they said there was absolutely no way. Howard said, 'Can I have a pep rally the night before a game?' They said yes, and we could have music. We drew 55,000, and Howard went up on the stage with the Beach Boys and the cheerleaders and we brought the team over on the bus. I remember the Beach Boys wanted organic carrots and the Commodores wanted ribs. We played Penn State the next day and beat them.

"The next year we had Jimmy Buffett, and then Howard left, and we didn't carry it on."

Sylvester Stallone Night

And another promotion: Sylvester "Rocky" Stallone Night. For the second home game in Schnellenberger's first season at Miami, the school decided to honor Stallone, an alumnus and the writer and star of *Rocky*, which won an Oscar for Best Picture.

Stallone showed up with then-girlfriend Susan Anton, but Hurricane football was still a tough sell. Attendance was announced at 20,069, but Hamlin thought about 12,000 showed up.

Longtime cheerleader Jim "The Yamma Yamma Man" Fleming remembered the game well. "I went to the school of communications with Sylvester Stallone," he said. "He has the same persona in real life as in *Rocky*, he's not acting. That's him. He sees me at the game and says, 'Yo, Yamma.'"

MAY THE FORCE BE WITH YOU

Whenever you see a Hurricanes head coach run off the field at the end of a game, you will see him being escorted by Ed Hudak, a backup defensive lineman during the Schnellenberger era who works for the Coral Gables police department. Since the late 1980s he has been in charge of security around the team at games and on road trips, and he serves as a liaison and consultant regarding law enforcement.

"It's been a lot of fun," said Hudak. "It's for a love of the alma mater. I had such great experiences through UM and met my wife there. The good part of my job is that I get to see a lot of my old buddies. I started this as a mentor program at the end of Jimmy's era, when there were more problems with the police. I brought the idea to Jimmy and Dennis, not saying the players need to be good boys but you're compounding your problems. A lot of the players have never talked to police. It started as a mentor role and advisory position, and it has grown to where a lot of these guys I can call friends. When they do dumb things they call me."

Hudak knows that college boys will be college boys. He was one of them as a Hurricane defensive lineman in the Schnellenberger era.

"When Howard came up with the idea of Building 36 [a dormitory] being the home for the football team, we had bed check every night," Hudak said. "The graduate assistants would be in charge. A couple of guys snuck out, and Howard put gates up. One night I was trying to sneak out, and as I was cutting out of my room, the G.A. yelled my name out. I told him I ran out of toilet paper. The only way to get out of that building was to get married. Nine guys got married in one year.

"My dad, who played football at Notre Dame, said, 'Son, do you want to be a big fish in a little pond or a little fish in a big pond?' And I came down to Miami. Assistant coaches Harold Allen and Bill Trout recruited me. Trout says, 'You'll play automatically. We're moving this guy to noseguard.' They had Burt and Lester Williams and Bob Nelson in the line, and I thought, 'I'm not sure how this is going to work out.' Everyone who started in front of me later started in the NFL. I realized what it's like to be a backup."

Spies at Practice

It's Dailey's and Hudak's job to keep the coach on time, coordinate travel plans with local police on road trips, and also make their presence known in hotel lobbies where the team stays.

"What I do day in and out is," Hudak said, "when kids have life questions about things like drivers' licenses, etc., I point them in the right direction. They're the only group I know that represents the university 24 hours a day. If they get in trouble, it's newsworthy."

One of Hudak's assignments has been to keep "spies" out of practice, especially back in the days when the team would practice on Friday at the site of a road game.

"We've had guys show up with binoculars," he said. "For years we would go to a game site and have Friday practice. They stopped that because it wasn't doing any good, and you couldn't put any new plays in.

"When we were doing the Friday thing, Butch would sit in the middle of an empty stadium and look at the top and see somebody. He'd say, 'Ed, who is that? You've got to find out who it is.' So I'd climb all the way to the top, and it would be the poor maintenance guy changing a lightbulb. We did it anyway, to put his mind at ease."

Almost Heaven

There's an old John Denver song called "Country Road" that has a line about "almost heaven ... West Virginia ... " But Morgantown, West Virginia, has at times been anything but heaven for the Hurricanes. The Mountaineers have some of the most raucous fans in all of sports.

One year after a Miami game, Hudak remembers seeing a little old lady standing by a rural road with an uplifted middle finger waiving at the team bus as it headed for the airport. "We'd get the finger a lot," he said.

"One year we had a Halloween game up there and I noticed this chain-link fence at the front of the stands and up the side. I went up to a major from the state police and asked him if the area was under construction. He said, 'No, that's where we put the students, or else they'll spill out all over.' I said, 'If the game is close or we win, we just let them come on down.' He said, 'There's 72,000 fans and that's bigger than any city in the state, and we can't hold them.'

"When Dennis Erickson was here and they beat us up there, I grabbed Dennis by the belt when the game ended. We didn't get to the sideline and they had already torn the goal posts down. I couldn't find West Virginia coach Don Nehlen and I said to Dennis, 'We've got to get out.' And kids were trying to punch Coach. They tore up our helmets and head sets. And assistant coach Randy Shannon was hit by a trash can from two stories up. I saw Nehlen afterwards and he said, 'I got off the field.'"

Another dangerous time Hudak remembered was at San Diego State during the Erickson era. "They wanted the state troopers to be in uniform and armed. A big fight broke out on the field, and we scored about two more times after that. One of their game operations people came over and pulled us aside and said someone called in a death threat to Coach Erickson and said if we scored again he'd be killed. We didn't want to stand near him. But nothing happened, it probably was some crank."

PLANES, NAILS AND ROOM SWITCHING

Hudak recalled several other tales:

"The funniest thing happened when we were going out to Arizona in 1994 to play Arizona State and the plane suddenly dropped about 300 feet," he said. "You could hear a pin drop. A couple of people banged heads on the ceiling but nobody was hurt. Talk about being scared. If the Miami Hurricanes ever looked like choir boys it was when that plane was coming down. A lot of guys were crossing themselves and saying, 'Amen, Jesus.'"

Over the years, Hudak has gotten to know several of the players well, especially the "characters."

"Warren Sapp was the leader on the team and in the locker room from early on," Hudak said. "One thing I admired is that he never changed who he is. Jerome Brown was just a funny, great kid and it was a tragedy when he was killed in a car crash. He had the mischievous smile all the time. He'd ride along on a big black bike and whitewall tires. Students were intimidated by him, but they misunderstood his goofing around. I'd get there and try to be mad at him and he'd start laughing, and I'd say, 'Go back to your room.'

"Cortez Kennedy was an intimidating individual, but one of the most affable. I remember when we were out in Pasadena and I was with my wife on Rodeo Drive, and she wanted to get her nails done. I looked across the street and saw Russell Maryland. He was having lunch and he smiled and came over and said, 'You're never going to hear the end of this. You're getting your nails done.'

"I also remember some players got into a fight one time at Big Daddy's on Coral Way after practice. Howard then announced that 'Big Daddy's is off limits. If I find anyone there, your butt is mine. Better give your soul to God, because your butt is mine.' He said it in that classic Howard voice.

"And I remember at the Peach Bowl at the end of the 1980 season. Jack Fernandez was my roommate on the road.

Howard's secretary was Mrs. Fernandez, and the rooms got switched, she got put in Jack's room. It came time for bed check and the G.A.'s banging on her door, yelling, 'You better open up the door!' I hear this lady screaming and I think, 'Oh, my God, Jack has a woman in the room.' When the door is finally opened, it's Coach's secretary. The next day Coach calls Jack down, and it was the first time I saw Howard smile in a long time."

THE TAMING OF A DOG

Howard Schnellenberger's search for a quarterback in 1982 took Miami recruiters from California to New York and included a stop at the Youngstown, Ohio, home of Bernie Kosar Jr.

"We're just ordinary people in Youngstown," said Bernie Kosar Sr. "Earl Morrall calls and he's one of the immortals, one of the legends. Here I am a 44-year-old kid who's impressed when the voice says, 'This is coach Earl Morrall calling.'

"Then when Coach Schnellenberger visited our home, it was awesome. He has charisma, magic. We have a cocker spaniel who barks at everyone who comes in the house, including me. But Schnellenberger was the first person he hasn't barked at. The man has magic."

The dog must have growled at coaches from Florida, West Virginia and Cincinnati because Kosar Jr. picked Miami over them. Or is the story just legend?

"I don't remember that happening," said Bernie Kosar Jr., who went on to help lead the Hurricanes to their first national championship in 1983. "It might have. But my dad takes after Coach Schnellenberger in the b.s. category."

Bernie Kosar

NEARLY LOST AT SEA

Two weeks before the start of the 1983 season, starting line-backer Danny Brown and starting offensive guard Juan Comendeiro went fishing with two friends in the Atlantic ocean and nearly lost their lives when the boat started sinking.

"We clung to the ice chest for like four to four and a half hours before we got picked up," said Brown. "We went out of Haulover Cut and went south and were 20 miles offshore. We were in a six-month-old 33-foot Chriscraft that had twin motors in the back. We were trying to catch a shark, and the line got wrapped up in the propeller. We cut the motor off and the boat turned toward the waves and had a low-cut transom. We couldn't see land or anything.

"I was thinking it was pretty much over with. I thought, 'Well, God, I guess you got me.'

"A fishing boat out of West Palm Beach rescued us. We ended up being rescued around Port Everglades. They called the Coast Guard, who picked us up. We took a taxi home, and that's the first time I went out by boat and came back by taxi.

"It was pretty wild. It was pretty scary. They claim to this day there were lifejackets on the boat. I don't know. I kind of helped the boat to sink because I was tearing it apart so fast and couldn't find them.

"Then all of a sudden I saw these boat bumpers floating out of the back of the boat and I saw the Igloo ice chest and grabbed it. Later on I wrote to Igloo and thanked them and they wrote something back and the president of the company said, 'Thanks for writing such a sincere letter, but at this time we don't endorse our product for lifesaving purposes. And have a good day.' And then they sent Mike O'Shea, our trainer, a bunch of Igloo coolers. But we didn't get one. Coach gave us a life jacket with a 'U' emblem on it. I outgrew that and gave it to some kid. After the season coach said, 'Don't let anybody have an accident. Juan and Danny come up, and here's your lifejack-ets.'

"We were very lucky. I couldn't swim too good.

"We went from almost dying to winning the national championship in one year. Life is pretty good."

THE MELTING POT

The national championship team in 1983 had only one returning starter on the offensive line, but they meshed well into what became known as the "Melting Pot" line. The starters: Canadian center Ian Sinclair; Cuban-American guard Juan Comendeiro; African-American guard Alvin Ward; Italian-American tackle Paul Bertucelli, and Irish-American tackle Dave Heffernan.

Comendeiro remembered several other wacky stories, including one that could have led to Vinny Testaverde transferring.

"One time we were coming back from the training table in the late afternoon after a mid-week practice in 1984," Comendeiro said. "Bernie Kosar was the starter and Vinny the backup. I saw Vinny at a pay phone and he hung up after talking to his family. He was upset that he was the backup and said, 'Hey, Juan, what do you think? I'm considering transferring.'

"I said, 'It was unfortunate he learned the offense faster. If he stays, you may not get a chance to play. And you'd be a starter anywhere else for sure. If I was as talented as you, I'd transfer.'

"The good part of the story is that he didn't listen to me. If he would have transferred, it would have left us with no quarterback. So this is my story about how good my opinion is. I've never been a Heisman Trophy winner and a multimillionaire. He's Superman, and he played several years in the NFL.

"One thing that made Michael Irvin fearless is that he didn't care. I remember when he was a freshman, at the training table, the seniors went to the front of the line. If a freshman was in front, they'd make him go to the back of the line. The whole offensive line came in at the same time, and Irvin was ahead of them and they asked him to move and he didn't budge. They had to physically grab him. He was going to fight the whole offensive line. Most guys would just say, 'Oh, yes sir, I'll go back.'"

On defensive lineman Jerome Brown: "He was playing on the scout team at a mid-week practice and I came up on a trap block from the left side to push him out. He came back behind me, kind of at half-speed, and he laid his shoulder down and I felt like I hit a wall. He was just pure talent, and he backed up his attitude. He was going full out on a half-effort drill.

"I remember another time when a backup offensive tackle got caught taking a loaf of bread and some meat home. The next day at practice Kim Helton, the offensive coordinator, made him wear the loaf of bread in practice tied to his belt. It was flapping up and down and it eventually broke and bread was all over.

"I also remember Howard's famous three-a-days as part of the championship season. It was legal then to have three practices. In the preseason we ran three miles at 5:30 in the morning with half pads, then full pads at 10.

"I was very fortunate. My goal all my career was never to make the Breakfast Club. They had to do monkey rolls, crab rolls and log rolls until they threw up. And gassers. There was no water during practice, and you couldn't take your helmet off. The Breakfast Club was for being late for a meeting, bad grades or missing curfew. You could have it for a week. There were always at least a dozen guys in it."

BUNCH OF MISFITS WITH HEART

The 1983 team was unranked at the beginning of the season, and it dropped the opening game at Florida 28-3. But it never lost again.

Linebacker Danny Brown on what made this team so special: "We had some good coaching. We were kind of like a bunch of misfits put together. We didn't have a whole lot of guys some of the other schools wanted. I guess we had a lot of heart. The coaches kind of got us in the right places, and we had guys step up and make big plays when they had to.

"I think when we beat Notre Dame and shut them out 20-0, it was a turning point. And the opening loss to Florida, the way the coaches handled that. We could have gone the other way. I thought they were going to come in and really get on us. It was a total flipflop the way they handled us, and everybody really responded to it. I think that was really a key to the whole year the way they handled us. We came back and won 11 in a row."

Players from that team were invited back to campus for a 20th reunion during the 2003 season. They were often asked if they felt like pioneers.

"I think we just have pride in knowing that we kind of got the thing started," Brown said. "There were a lot of good players here before we got here, and there were a lot of good coaches before we got here. We kind of built a foundation that made this a great program."

He added, "I don't think I'll ever forget Kenny Calhoun at the end of the game against Nebraska. His fingertip touched the ball to break up their two-point conversion, and we won 31-30. I was on that side and I think the quarterback could have walked in. They took me out of the play. I was on the ground pretty much because the fullback got me. Everything's kind of got to be in the right place at the right time. That's kind of how a lot of things went for us. The small things really do matter."

HEADLINE: BRAINS AND BRAWN

While many players take five years to earn a degree, Kosar needed only three while pursuing a double major in finance and economics. He was the starter for the 1983 national champions and again in 1984 before moving on to the NFL.

Stephen Sapp, professor and chairman of the Department of Religious Studies at UM, served as an honorary faculty coach for the Mississippi State game in Starkville in 1983. He saw firsthand how Kosar's classroom smarts carried over to football.

"My job was to carry the headset wire for Howard Schnellenberger, which meant I was privy to all the conversations between him and quarterbacks coach Marc Trestman," Sapp recalled. "At one point in the game, Bernie looked over for the play call and Trestman started signaling it in. Obviously before he was finished Bernie turned back to the huddle and Trestman said to Howard, 'Coach, that kid is scary he's so smart. I think he knows what play we're going to call before we do.'"

CHAPTER 6

Becoming America's Hip Team

OVERCOATS AND TOUPEES

If they ever conduct a poll on who is the best storyteller in the University of Miami football program, assistant head coach Art Kehoe probably will win. That might be because he has been the most visible weaver of tales in recent years.

If you poll longtime observers of the program, Bill Trout and the late Walt Kichefski likely would challenge Kehoe in the voting. Trout and Kichefski, like Kehoe, played at Miami and served as assistant coaches for several years.

Following are several tales courtesy of Trout, who served as an assistant from 1976 through 1984:

• "Ron Marciniak came to Lou Saban's staff from the University of Dayton. He went from Division III to I and did not stop at II. He was an offensive line coach and had a Catholic-school mentality. He was used to a tight budget. We had big-time recruits come in and he'd take them to Lums, the hot dog place, for dinner for a 39-cent hotdog.

"It got to the point where the rental agency wouldn't rent cars to him because he crashed them. He'd scout opponents, and in those days he had to wait for the film to bring it back. One time he he took the film and threw it in the trunk. He didn't realize it went into the tire well, and they had to get a welder to get it out.

"He was coaching running backs, including Ottis Anderson, and they couldn't eat at the training table because he'd see them and put down salt and pepper shakers and run plays. One time they took so long they got locked in and couldn't get out. They had to get the campus security to get them out."

• "Howard Schnellenberger and assistant coach Chris Vagotis were in Pittsburgh recruiting. It used to be a big deal that the last plane out of Pittsburgh would be at midnight and then there were none 'til morning. They were running late and Howard said to Chris, 'Turn the car in, and I'll check us in.' So Howard went to the gate and got on the plane, and Chris wasn't there yet. Howard was smoking his pipe as they shut the door, and Chris showed up and Howard waved to him. Chris called me and said, 'What do I do now?'"

• "We were in Chicago with Howard recruiting. It was cold in January, below zero. We met in the lobby of the hotel and we were going to a kid's home early in the evening. I had a huge overcoat and Howard just had a suit. He said, 'Nah, it isn't that cold.'

"I took the overcoat off and put it between us in the car. We got to the kid's house and parked on the street, and the house was back about 40 yards. Howard got out of the car and put on the coat and was walking up the hill. We got to the kid's door and I was freezing to death, and Howard said, 'Coach Trout, don't you know any better to wear a coat? I told you to wear a coat.'"

• "In Jimmy's first year, Bruce Mays was the administrative assistant and he wore a hairpiece, and it was cheap looking. His office was across from mine. He had a sign on his door that would have the 'Word For The Day.' Players took it as a joke more than learning. Kyle Vanderwende, one of the quarterbacks, had a dry sense of humor. We were going on the road and Bruce was sitting on the bus and Bruce got on the bus, and then Kyle got on and looked at Bruce and said, 'Hey, Coach, the word for today is toupee,' and he kept walking. Bruce turned red, and we couldn't help but laugh."

FLYING PROJECTOR

More tales from Trout:
• "Lou Saban was looking at film and had the offensive team in there. Lou could lose his temper, and he was getting madder at the backs. Kenny Johnson was missing blocks and Lou was hollering at them. Lou picked up the film projector and threw it, and it hit Ottis Anderson but didn't hurt him. The projector cost $1,200, and Ottis was the only offensive weapon we had. Lou said, 'I don't give a damn.'"

• "Lou had just come to Miami, and Harry Mallios was the athletic director and Art Lasky was the ticket guy and handled finances for checks. We wanted to go recruiting, and Lou told Art he needed a $2,000 check for each coach on Friday so they could go recruiting on Monday. At dinner at the training table, Lasky showed up with a bag filled with $20 bills. I always wondered what big-time athletics was all about."

• "We were having a recruiting meeting with Lou, and each coach was going over his best recruits and their attributes and who else was recruiting him. Rick Lantz, a defensive coach, kept saying, 'It's us and somebody else, it's us and somebody else.' Lou says, 'Remind me to not schedule 'Somebody Else,' because they're going to have a helluva team in a couple of years.'"

• "We were playing Florida one year when Lou was here and they were using SEC officials. Assistant coach Arnie Romero and Lou thought they cheated us. They called a 15-yard penalty on Don Latimer and another 15-yarder. Lou then yelled to the officials, 'The next SOB who calls 15 yards, I'm coming on the field and putting my foot on the ball, and this game ain't starting anymore.'"

• "We went to Houston in Howard's first year and the equipment manager was a guy who'd forget stuff. We called him Number 9. He got the name because he forgot to pack nine jerseys for the Houston trip. Bill Yeoman was the coach at Houston, and Howard asked him for nine white practice jerseys with certain numbers, and they were red numbers. The equipment guy also forgot some of the coaches' shoes, and assistant coach Harold Allen had to wear cowboy boots."

A HELICOPTER AND PETE'S HILL

When Miami played Nebraska in the 1984 Orange Bowl Classic for the national title, Schnellenberger found a novel way to cope with the traffic: Go over it.

"We practiced at the campus and stayed on Miami Beach," said Trout. "The traffic was brutal. Howard got use of a helicopter to save time. On Media Day, Nebraska practiced first, and Howard said to keep the kids in the locker room so they couldn't mess with Nebraska. So the kids stayed in the locker room, Nebraska was finishing and they were taking pictures, and this helicopter came out of the sky and landed in the Orange Bowl. Everybody came over and shook his hand.

"He did the greatest psychological job to get our kids ready to play. He said, 'There are going to be things said in the media by me and others, and just ignore it. They say they are 17 points better. Horse[censored]. They say they're the best team in the last 50 years. Horse[censored].' He made about 50 statements and they all ended with 'horse[censored].' The kids would go around saying, 'Horse[censored].'"

And more Trout tales:

• "When Carl Selmer was head coach, I took the freshman team to The Bahamas to play the Bahamian All-Stars at the

Princess Something complex. We stayed at the Holiday Inn, and we were there a couple days when something told me I should check on the pregame meal. They had planned fish and grits. I said, 'No, no, that's not going to work.' They had 77 guys, and every team had a different color jersey. They told us to wear white.

"It got so bad, it was 31-0 at the end of the first quarter. Mike Archer was my defensive coordinator, and I would tell him, 'Don't rush the punter and don't return any more points. Tell the kick returner to signal for a fair catch.' One time we didn't rush and they didn't run downfield, so the kid caught the ball and ran. He said, 'I forgot, Coach.' I said, 'What the [censored]' and got a 15-yard penalty for cussing. It was the only bowl game we'd been in for years."

•   "Pete Elliott made a putting and chipping green near the end of one of the practice fields. They called it Pete's Hill. That's when I knew football wasn't very important at Miami. I wondered if Bear Bryant had one of these at Tuscaloosa. It took 15 yards away from our field.

"We had no money. I remember Howard sent out a memo that said coffee cups could only be half-filled, because if they spilled we couldn't afford to shampoo the carpet."

•   "Suzy Wilkoff was the first female recruiting coordinator in college football. She tried to be a mother and big sister to these kids. In 1983, a week before we were going to play Florida, Suzy quit. Howard pulled me out of my meeting with the outside linebackers and said, 'You're now the recruiting coordinator. You're going to coach and recruit.' We had no computers back then, so we mailed stuff to kids every week. We had orange lists and green lists and sent cards on their birthdays and mailograms before big games wishing them luck. I'd be there until 10:30 at night with football stuff and then stay 'til two on recruiting stuff and be back at six."

•   "Saban was always changing the time of games. I'll never forget the time a staff meeting was breaking up and we were walking down the hall, and one secretary said, 'Coach Saban,

Mr. So and So wants to know what time is the game.' Lou replies, 'Ask him what time he can be there.'"

• "Lou had a surprise birthday party. He didn't care for Art Lasky, who was in charge of finance and tickets and getting people in stadium. [Assistant coach] Billy Proulx and I bought a toilet seat and wrapped it up for a gift. On the lid when it was folded down we had written, 'Lou, thanks for filling the bowl.' And we had a picture of Lasky on the inside."

• "Scott Atwell was from my hometown of Key West, and I got him a scholarship in the sports information department through sports information director George Gallet. Scott played freshman football at Miami, and the rule was that if you played in a freshman game, you couldn't play in the varsity game that week. All our quarterbacks were hurt, and Scott was a freshman in the sports information department and was bragging about being a quarterback and throwing to Speedy Neal in Key West. John Smantana, a defensive back who had played quarterback in high school, was the only guy available, and Howard said we had to have another in case he got hurt. So I got Scott, and he weighed only 141 pounds. Howard made him dress out for the Florida game, I thought Howard was kidding. Smatana did get hurt, but after a timeout Smatana came around in time.

• "Mike Rodrigue was our starting quarterback in 1978 and early in '79. In high school at Choctawhatchee, I recruited him and he was a real good athlete, and his dad had played at FSU. I was in the press box at one of his games and nobody around me wanted the kid to go to Miami. One redneck with a southern accent said, 'What position are you recruiting that boy to play?' I said, 'We'll give him a shot at quarterback.' The guy said, 'You're a big guy. What you know about quarterback?' I said, 'I've never been an egg, but I know an omelette when I see one.'"

JOGGING MEMORY LANE

No journalist has covered University of Miami athletics longer than Edwin Pope, longtime *Miami Herald* sports editor and columnist. He has chronicled everything from the strong teams of the mid-1950s to the up-and-down '60s, to the turbulent '70s and the emergence of the program as the dominant force in college football.

"My best memory by far is the 1983 season's Orange Bowl game," Pope recalls. "When I first came here in 1956, they were pretty good. But as time went along and they fell on hard times and were underfunded and unequipped, the worst time of week was going out to UM. I thought there were times in late '60s and early '70s that they didn't try that hard. I remember All-America offensive tackle Dennis Harrah one year commiserating after a game and he said, 'The coaches sort of act like it doesn't make any difference whether we win or not.'

"I guess the player I remember most fondly is Bernie Kosar. I had breakfast with him the week before he started his first game against Florida in 1983. They didn't win but he played a great game, and I wrote a column saying that even though they got beat, they found a quarterback to lead them. People always write about his lousy form, but he was a great credit for the university. I remember when he left after the Fiesta Bowl in 1985, I said something to him in the locker room about whether he'd leave or not. He said, 'It doesn't matter whether I leave or not. The program's in good hands.' I liked the classy way he handled things. He'd call you up to meet his parents and little brother."

FOURTEEN HEAD COACHES

Miami has hired 14 head football coaches during the years Edwin Pope has covered the team. He got to know all of them well.

"I admired Howard Schnellenberger and I still do," he said. "I remember going out there after his terrible decision to resign after the 1983 national championship and go to the USFL. I said, 'It's not going to be the same.' He said, 'It never is.'

"When Jimmy Johnson replaced him, I had sort of an awkward situation, because I liked Bill Trout. Unfortunately he and Jimmy were on different sides, and Miami forced Jimmy to keep his assistants from Howard's staff. When Tom Olivadotti quit, Trout became defensive coordinator, and it was a mess, especially the last three games against Maryland, Boston College and UCLA in the Fiesta Bowl. I was going to track Jimmy until he left the stadium at the Fiesta Bowl, and he said one epithet over and over for a least an hour until he got in the car with his wife. He looked at the ground and up at sky, and I'm sure he was thinking what a mess it was."

The Boston College game was marked by the infamous "Hail Flutie" pass by Heisman Trophy winner Doug Flutie on the final play to beat the Hurricanes 47-45 in the Orange Bowl.

"Tolbert Bain, Darrell Fullington and Selwyn Brown were back there covering in the end zone," Pope recalled. "I was as shocked as they were. I was standing on the sideline near the end zone and thought, 'Don't let him [receiver Gerald Phelan] get behind you,' and he got behind them. One of the few hard things I've ever done in the newspaper business was that I had to write about the game and I had the break on the story of Trout quitting after the game, and it didn't come out well. Twenty-one years later Flutie was still running around in the NFL like a 17-year-old. Miami wasn't the last to feel the sting of Flutie."

Jimmy Johnson

Schnellenberger's move to the ill-fated USFL fell through, and he took the head job at the University of Louisville, where he turned around that program and beat Alabama in the Fiesta Bowl. Pope continued to admire Schnellenberger's successes.

"Art Modell was getting ready to hire a new coach for the Cleveland Browns, and Howard was at Louisville," Pope recalled, "and Art asked me about people. I said, 'Howard's the best. He never gives up on anything.'"

TARGET ON THEIR CHEST

Alonzo Highsmith started at fullback for three years (1984-86) and contributed as a freshman on the 1983 national champion team. He was Miami's leading rusher (50 yards in seven carries) and scored a touchdown in the Orange Bowl victory over Nebraska.

"In 1983 I saw that this team was special," said Highsmith. "My senior class of 27 or 30 guys, we were all similar, we had the same attitudes. Our freshman year we went to the movies and saw *Kujo*, about some St. Bernard that went crazy. Then the whole freshman class went crazy.

"If you saw one Cane you saw them all. We galvanized the city. We were a highly recruited class and were from different parts of town. Melvin Bratton was from Northwestern High School and he was the 'mayor' of that part of town. Bennie Blades was from Fort Lauderdale and was 'mayor' of the north, and I came from down south and I was the top guy for that area. We all brought a segment of the area into the program. Never before had Miami had that many top recruits from the area.

"By the end of my freshman year, Miami became a hip place to go. People saw the smoke coming out of the tunnel, saw the high-fives and the pointing fingers. All of a sudden everyone in America wanted to beat us. We put a target on our chests. Michael Irvin high-fiving would tick everybody off. When you talk loud, you had a lot to back up. So we had to play."

Highsmith is now a college scout for the Green Bay Packers, and he sees the program from a different perspective. "I didn't realize the effect Miami had on college football, the bravado of it. Miami brought a lot to college football in 20 years."

Alonzo Highsmith

WHAT'S UP, DOC?

Father Leo Armbrust, former team chaplain, remembers the time when Dr. John Cunio, one of the team physicians for several years, said that "football may not necessarily build character, but it will always reflect it." Armbrust added, "Before the Nebraska game in Orange Bowl for the 1983 national title, Cunio walked up to defensive lineman Tony Fitzpatrick and said, 'If you guys win this game, you guys can have my Porsche.' After the game was over Fitz walked over and said, 'Hey, Doc, where are the keys to your Porsche?' Cunio said, 'I checked into it, Tony, I can't give it to you because it's an NCAA violation.'"

Armbrust added, "The relationship a lot of players have had with doctors like John Uribe, Richard Mariani and Robert

Tanner, that's stability and permanency. Since 1983, the only head trainers have been Mike O'Shea, Kevin O'Neill, Andy Clary, Todd Toriscelli, Scott McGonagle and Andreu Swasey. They've been able to maintain that sense of family."

LEAVING IT ON THE FIELD

Even Jim Fleming, the ageless cheerleader known as the Yamma Yamma Man, had to be carried off the field after the first Miami-Nebraska national title game.

"It was a highly emotionally charged game, and all week I was at all the functions, the tailgating and pep rallies," said Fleming. "An hour before the game, normally my routine is to warm up myself downfield and do a few stretches, smell the field and look at the stands and get my game face on. Only a handful of fans usually are there at that time. I ran out of the tunnel and a tremendous sound startled me. I was shocked; the stands were virtually full. I realized I was the only orange thing coming out of the tunnel, and the emotion of the crowd rolled out on me. It was a feeling like the Pope and rock stars must get. Me and 80,000 of my friends. I started dancing on the Orange Bowl symbol and did 'Let's Go, Canes.' By the time the kickoff was ready, I was exhausted. I left it all on the field before the game.

"Also, I sprained my ankle badly in the first half, because I wore myself out. The trainer, Mike O'Shea, taped me at the half, and I took pain pills. In the fourth quarter my ankle was swelling, but the show must go on. I was right there near the end zone for the tipped pass [when Nebraska's two-point conversion pass was broken up by Ken Calhoun], but I was in la la land by that time. I kept afloat by adrenaline. After that play I went down on my knees and face, and I was deliriously happy."

He continued to be an on-field cheerleader until the mid-1990s. "I made my own decision to retire," Fleming said. "My wife got tired of me coming home and collapsing."

Yamma Meets 2-Bits

The University of Florida has its version of the Yamma Yamma Man. Known as Mr. 2-Bits, he works the crowd from the stands or on the field into a frenzy with an animated version of the old cheer: "Two bits, four bits, six bits, a dollar ..."

In Gainesville there's a bar called 2-Bits, and Jim Fleming ended up there one night.

"We heard people singing 'Night of a Thousand Dances' that goes 'Na, na na na na, na na na na ...' and we're right in the middle of a Gator rally. I said, 'They stole my thing that we do in Miami.' So we went inside and suddenly I'm face to face with Mr. 2-Bits. He's really a nice guy, and he said, 'I want you to do '2-Bits' with me.' So I got to do 2-Bits with Mr. 2-Bits at 2-Bits Bar."

Midseason Bowl Game

Ron Steiner, the sports information director for Howard Schnellenberger, recalled how the 1983 home game against Notre Dame not only served as the turning point in the first national championship season but also served as a midseason version of a bowl game.

"CBS had told Miami in the summer they'd televise the game nationally in prime time, the only one of the year," Steiner said. "We had six months' notice and put together The Magic of Miami Festival, and the Orange Bowl Committee was the producer. They had a giant pyrotechnic display in the end zone, and the city was involved in lighting up downtown buildings. We got 12 minutes of the halftime, and that's probably never happened since for a regular-season game, because networks just don't give you 12 minutes of halftime. It became a community event to promote the city. Howard was always tying the two together—whatever is good for the city, and vice versa. We had a nine o'clock kickoff, and nobody did that back then. Everything was perfect. We had festivals the whole week.

"The classic thing that happened the night of the game was that the weather turned windy, and when they lit the giant pyrotechnic sign that said, 'MIAMI IS FOR ME,' the burning embers cascaded down because of the wind and landed onto fur coats, leather coats and Lincoln Continentals. We had to pay for a lot of fur coats and paint jobs.

"We had a halftime show that's reserved for bowl games. And we won the game 20-0. It was no contest. It was amazing to have that opportunity. Coach's whole mindset was to play whoever, whenever, and let's make something out of it.

"That was the last time a team used TV to blatantly boost a city. And it was a $100,000 expense the city had to raise. We thought if we get whupped, at least the city will win. There was no ESPN coverage to the degree that there is now. How terrible it would have been if the cameras would have looked down and there was an empty stadium [attendance was 52,480]. It was scripted and was called the Classic College Football Weekend."

Steiner said that when the network cameras came into the Orange Bowl, "They booted out the local TV. The only place to go was on the roof, but the forecast was for rain. In our efforts to take care of the press, we were frantic. The Orange Bowl Committee was supposed to build something up there, but it didn't happen. So we sent Scot Atwell from our staff to Sears with a credit card, and he bought a tent, and we were going to strap it down with duct tape. He got back a couple of hours before the game, and as he was tying it, a gust of wind came up and he nearly became the first parasailer into Biscayne Bay from the roof of the Orange Bowl."

DISAPPEARING ACT

Because the Hurricanes struggled to draw big crowds for games other than Florida and Notre Dame in the 1970s and early 1980s, a large ticket department wasn't needed. But as Ron Steiner recalled, the office occasionally became overwhelmed when the Hurricanes began to pile up victories in the 1980s.

"Charlie Gesino and Mary May Burruss were the only full-time people in the ticket office," Steiner said. "They had to deal with ticket sales until the day of the game. In 1981 the volume for midweek ticket sales soared when Penn State, the number-one team in the country, came to Miami. It was just Burruss and maybe a student intern in the office, and that was it. And that was the only place you could buy tickets in advance.

"All of sudden we saw an ambulance outside the building. As Mary May was waiting on a customer, she disappeared behind the counter. There was a line of people, and she was lying on the ground passed out. She did recover but was never quite the same. We had no depth in the ticket office."

CAN YOU HEAR ME NOW?

Before the Hurricanes started competing for national championships, budgets were extremely tight. In fact, things got so tight in May of 1983 that coaches were calling recruits from pay phones.

"I remember seeing Tom Olivadotti calling recruits with quarters from the lobby of the Hecht Athletic Center because the school wouldn't let us make long-distance calls," Steiner said. "Here's the defensive coordinator standing in the noisy lobby—clink, clink, clink—calling recruits. They put out directives that there would be no more long-distance calls until the budget year ended in June. But you can't stop calling recruits, and this was before there were cell phones."

LOCK-DOWN PRACTICE

Though most practices have been closed to the public and media in recent years, that was seldom the case when the program was growing into a national power. Ron Steiner recalled an exception.

"In the spring of 1984 after the championships and before Howard Schnellenberger left for the pro thing," Steiner said, "the team had a bad case of being spoiled and the big head from the championship. We went on busses to Lockhart Stadium in Fort Lauderdale for a scrimmage, and at halftime he put them on the bus and took them home.

"He told the crowd, 'Thanks for coming,' and told the players, 'Get your butts on the bus, we're going back to practice. And don't take off your equipment.'

"They had the only closed practice I ever knew of. It was a lock down. Karl Schmitt [assistant sports information director] told the Miami media that practice was closed, and they wouldn't take no for an answer. We put padlocks on the gates, and the windscreens were up. But there was a dumpster up against the wall, and one of the TV guys got on the dumpster, and soon they had a mini-press box up there—*National Enquirer* kind of coverage."

Art Kehoe, a graduate assistant coach on that team, remembered "the defense kicking the crap out of the offense. At halftime Howard was livid. I was in charge of the training table, and he said to me, 'Tell them we'll be late. Tell them to fix something that stays warm for a long time.' We had a 103-play scrimmage, and that was after running 50 before."

CHAPTER 7

Building a Dynasty

EXTRA! READ ALL ABOUT IT!

The hiring of Jimmy Johnson as Miami coach in 1984 began with meetings in Dallas. UM officials hoped to keep the coaching search as private as possible, but they ended up being scooped by a newspaper reporter before the final deal was done. Ron Stone, a member of the coaching search committee, remembers it well.

"I called Paul Dee, who was the school's legal counsel then, and we got to the Dallas Hyatt. We walked in there, and what I didn't know was that Richie Rosenblatt of the *Miami News* was over there in the corner on the phone. Athletic director Sam Jankovich was in the lobby waiting for us to show up. Richie saw me show up, and Sam went hiding behind a pole, and Richie saw this and started following us around for the next 48 hours.

"At the end of it all, we left Dallas and came back to Miami. We'd done the deal, and now we had to convene a meeting of the UM executive board of trustees and the president at Neil Schiff's house. We arranged all this en route. We got back here about 5:30, and the meeting was at six o'clock Monday afternoon. Sam had somebody pick us up at the airport. Jimmy wasn't with us, he had gone back to Oklahoma State to tell his team. He was going to come back the next day when we had the press conference.

"We were driving down LeJeune road from the airport and we got to the traffic light at Bird Road by Coral Gables High School. And as we were sitting at the traffic light on the way to this meeting, the afternoon *Miami News* was still running. The kids used to hawk them at street corners. And this kid walked by the car with a bunch of newspapers, and the banner across the top of the newspaper reads, 'Miami Hires Jimmy Johnson.' And I just happened to see it and I say, 'Oh, my God, look at this! Kid, give me this!' Richie broke the story before we had a chance to meet with and tell the president and the board who it was. He went way out on a limb with that banner, but he had it right."

THE RECRUITING MACHINE

When Jimmy Johnson was hired in June of 1984, he was under orders to retain everyone from Howard Schnellenberger's staff who wanted to stay. All but one did, and Johnson's lone hiring turned out to be fortuitous.

"After we completed that hire," Stone recalled, "Jimmy's wife, Linda Kay, went back to Stillwater to sell the house. Sam went back to the northwest for a vacation, and Paul went on a cruise. Jimmy was here with nobody he knew other than me. We spent every evening together that summer. At the beginning of that he really focused on what to do with the staff he inherited. We arranged for him to live temporarily in a suite at the Mutiny Hotel. We'd meet there and talk about every possible thing, including the program and staff. The only position he had an opportunity to fill was defensive coordinator, because

Tom Olivadotti left in frustration and went to work for Don Shula with the Miami Dolphins. He had two mishaps. He brought in two defensive coordinators he knew well and they didn't work out. And he was getting frustrated with the process. One day he says, 'I've figured this thing out, I've decided to name Bill Trout as coordinator and bring in a guy who I should've brought in in the first place from Oklahoma State who is full of fire and is an absolute recruiting machine, what I really need. His name is Butch Davis. I'm heading to the airport to pick him up, and he has no place to stay. Do you think he could bunk out at that extra house you have over by the university?' I said, 'Absolutely.' He brought Butch back, and I invited him to stay with me for the balance of the summer."

Davis served as defensive line coach under Johnson at Miami from 1984-88 and went with Johnson to the Dallas Cowboys in 1989. When Dennis Erickson left Miami for the Seattle Seahawks, Dee hired Davis to guide the program through the pending NCAA sanctions and new glory days.

Never Leave a Game Early

Walt Kichefski, the longtime assistant coach known as the ultimate Gator hater, missed one of the greatest Hurricane moments in the rivalry because he left the game early. It happened when Miami and Florida met early in the 1984 season at Tampa Stadium.

Quarterback Kerwin Bell led the Gators to a touchdown and a 20-19 lead with 41 seconds left. That didn't faze Bernie Kosar, who led the Hurricanes 72 yards in five plays to the go-ahead touchdown. Then on the game's final play, Miami cornerback Tolbert Bain intercepted a Bell pass and returned it 50 yards for the third touchdown in 41 seconds as Miami won 32-20.

"Walter and I drove up in his motor home, and my wife, Kathy, and his wife, Helene, had press box tickets," recalled former player and longtime board of trustees member Don Marriutto Sr. "I didn't have press box tickets, so Walt and I sat in the stands. He left the game early, dejected, and got to the motorhome and didn't know we won the game.

"I said, 'What's the matter?' He said, 'We had it won and lost it.'

"I thought he was joking, but he was dead serious. I had to turn the radio on to convince him. Then he was jubilant. He started watching replays on TV and was the happiest guy in world. We never let him forget that."

BERNIE HAS "THE GIFT"

Early in 1985, Ron Stone received a call from Marc Trestman, Miami's quarterbacks coach. "He said, 'Ron, could you meet for breakfast? I have something to discuss that's very important.' We met at the Holiday Inn across from the university. Marc said, 'I'm going to be leaving. I finished law school, and Bud Grant offered me a full-time job with the Vikings with their quarterbacks. I played at Minnesota, and I'm from that area. It's just a great opportunity. But that's not what I want to talk about. It's our quarterbacks. If there's anything that you guys can do within the rules to keep Bernie here, you've got to do it.'

"I said, 'What do you mean?' Marc said, 'Get him an apartment on Key Biscayne, something within the rules. Have him use one more year of eligibility, because he's going to walk away with two years of eligibility left.'

"I said, 'But you've been telling me the guy behind him is probably better than him.'

"'That's right. Vinny's going to be a show unto himself. But Bernie's got the gift.'

"'The gift? What do you mean?'

"Marc said, 'If you or I are out there on the field and we're up over center and we take the snap and backpedal and watch everything unfold at a thousand miles an hour and sort it out to make the right decision and hope not to throw to the other team, Vinny is like that. But Bernie's different, he has the gift. When he backpedals from center, to him it looks like it's unfolding in slow motion. That's the gift, and almost nobody has that. But if it doesn't happen, Vinny will be a great player.'"

Miami didn't keep Kosar, who had been redshirted his freshman season and started in the 1983 and 1984 seasons. He earned his degree in business in three years and was selected by his home area Cleveland Browns in the first round of the NFL supplemental draft in the summer of 1985. Testaverde went on to win the Heisman Trophy in 1986.

HAIL FLUTIE

The premier college quarterbacks of 1984—Bernie Kosar and soon-to-be-named Heisman Trophy winner Doug Flutie and Bernie Kosar—matched up in the Orange Bowl the day after Thanksgiving. Though it was cool and rained much of the game, the weather didn't hamper the game. Kosar completed 25 of 38 passes for 447 yards and two touchdowns. Flutie connected on 34 of 46 passes for 472 yards and three touchdowns.

Kosar's passing set up a one-yard run by Melvin Bratton for a touchdown and a 45-41 lead with 28 seconds left. Flutie calmly moved his team to midfield, and on the final play heaved a prayer that was answered when flanker Gerard Phelan caught the ball in a crowd in the end zone for a 48-yard touchdown and a 47-45 victory.

Phelan broke past the secondary and, while falling backward into the end zone, clutched the ball that sailed over the fingertips of Darrell Fullington and Tolbert Bain. It became known as the Hail Flutie pass.

"I remember being on the field standing on the goal line during the Boston College game," said Rich Dalrymple, assistant sports information director at that time. "We announced there were 26,000 there, and probably 260,000 swear they were there. It was cold and windy and was the day after Thanksgiving. We'd always go down to the field, sports information director Karl Schmitt and I, as publicists do as time is running out. We were saying, 'OK, we'll bring Jimmy into the interview room. Should we bring Bernie and Melvin?' It would be such a thrilling win and a lot media were there—Dick Schaap and a lot of high-powered people. We had it all mapped out. Then we saw this pass kind of fall out of the sky and we were thinking, 'Well this is the last one.' And Gerald Phelan came out of the pile with the ball. And Karl said, 'OK, what are we going to do now?'

"The door to the locker room stayed closed a long time, even to us. One time Jimmy waved Karl in and said the players didn't want the media to come in. We knew we couldn't do that, regardless. We enlisted Father Leo as a mediator and he negotiated after the long delay.

"Finally the door opened, and Bernie was the first to step up and address how disappointed they were. It was truly a devastating game in the middle of what was as difficult and frustrating a period as I had experienced there."

John Routh, a.k.a. the Ibis mascot, concurred. "I'd bring a bag of props to the games and had grabbed a bag and was walking toward the locker room. I sat the bag down and stood up on a bench. I saw the pass and saw the celebration and literally stood there five minutes. We assumed we'd won the game. It was like watching your whole world crumble in front of you."

Bill Trout, Miami's defensive coordinator, announced his resignation after the game. He had planned to resign regardless of the outcome.

"Butch Davis [defensive line coach] was down on the sideline and hooked to me on the phone," Trout said. "Butch asked me what defense to run, and I said, 'Run a prevent. Let's do this because Flutie can run around. If they get a great return, we'll play a regular defense.' So they returned it not very far, normal, and we played the prevent. Everybody was in unison with it.

"Flutie had done that earlier in the season, and we practiced against the Hail Mary. Their touchdown didn't come out anything different, Darrell Fullington just misjudged the ball.

"Somebody made a statement that we weren't in the press box for that play. They hold the elevators for coaches, and if you are not on it, they go down. The offensive coaches left because they scored. Donny Soldinger and Danny Brown and maybe one other guy and I remained. Who in their right mind would leave the press box with the Heisman trophy winner on the field? There was no confusion on what defense we would use. We stayed to the last play and walked down the whole stairs. We were the last ones in the locker room.

"During the week I was interviewed by ESPN and said that both offenses are very explosive. And the guy asked me how you stop them. I said you don't stop them, but you try to slow them down. I said I wouldn't be surprised if this came down to whoever had the ball in their hands last."

JIMMY'S REVENGE

Before Jimmy Johnson became coach at Miami, he was interested in the head coaching job at his alma mater, Arkansas. Things didn't work out with the Razorbacks, who hired Lou Holtz, but Johnson had a chance to send a message to his old school when the Hurricanes played at Arkansas in 1987.

"He really wanted to get that head coaching job at Arkansas," said team chaplain Father Leo Armbrust. "For whatever reason he didn't get it. I don't know if he was aware of it, but some of his assistant coaches, Gary Stevens in particular, stood up the week of the game and told the team how important it was to play for Jimmy, because he had really wanted that job.

"The team truly played with a purpose. It was so evident when it manifested in a 31-0 Miami lead at halftime. We came in the locker room at halftime, and usually the board is covered with changes and formations we need to make or need to attack. When we came in, not one play offensively or defensively was on the chalk board to go over. Only three words: MAINTAIN YOUR INTENSITY."

The Hurricanes did, as they won 51-7.

THE HEART AND SOUL

Rich Dalrymple, a member of the sports information staff from 1984 until joining Jimmy Johnson at Dallas in 1990, credited defensive tackle Jerome Brown as being "the guy, the granddaddy for establishing a tone, a mindset and an attitude on the team. When Jerome said something, it was not questioned and everyone followed in suit, including Jimmy Johnson. When Jerome said, 'We're wearing fatigues,' everybody said, 'OK.' And Jimmy said, 'If that's what you want, OK.'

"Jerome was the heart and soul of the Hurricanes' mindset of being flamboyant and confident, and to a certain extent that arrogance UM fans loved and the rest of the country started to dislike. Then you had personalities who enforced it, like Michael Irvin, Alonzo Highsmith and Melvin Bratton."

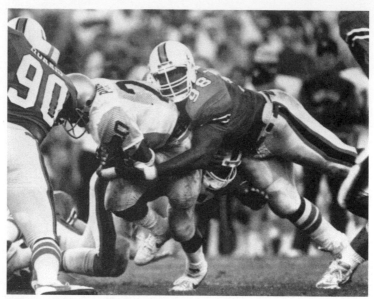

Jerome Brown

Rough Transition

The Hurricanes labored through a difficult transition season in 1984 when Johnson replaced Schnellenberger. Dalrymple recalled that "we were 8-2 and almost in the hunt for the national championship. If anybody would have a shot at the national title with two losses—we'd lost to Michigan and Florida State early—it would have been us. The game prior to the Hail Flutie one we were leading 31-0 at the half against Maryland and lost 42-40.

"I remember seeing Edwin Pope after the game saying, 'I've never seen anything like this in my life.'

"It seemed that we had survived all the bumps and had to inherit almost the entire staff and were coming off a Cinderella season. We opened up against Auburn and Bo Jackson in the Kickoff Classic. There were probably more first-round draft choices in that game than any other. Then we faced Kerwin Bell's first start for Florida at Tampa, and then lost to Michigan. Then Bobby Bowden was throwing gadget plays when we got off the bus [in a 38-3 Florida State victory at the Orange Bowl]. Then things got hairy. The talent offensively was so strong, and the defense was not the same one that Jimmy ran at Oklahoma State. Miami was using a 5-2 and he was a 4-4 guy. It was very awkward, and we're sitting 8-2 and have a chance at a big bowl game. Then Bill Trout quit as defensive coordinator and we had to play in the Fiesta Bowl. In the aftermath of that 39-37 loss to UCLA there were serious rumblings that this program is going to hell just because of a transition, and Howard was almost perceived as a saint because of his years leading up to that. And we

Vinny Testaverde

were playing a schedule that would make it difficult to repeat no matter who was coach.

"Then we lost the 1985 opener to Florida and then the streak [31 regular-season victories] began. The Florida game was Vinny's first start, but he was impressive and he had three sophomore receivers in Brett Perriman, Brian Blades and Michael Irvin. That was probably the first indication of the program being at the level where you just plug the next guy in and he may be better than the guy he replaced.

"With the Orange Bowl win over Oklahoma for the 1987 national championship, a huge weight was lifted off Jimmy's shoulders. He didn't put the critics to bed until that victory."

IMAGE BATTLES

With success came scrutiny. Before the Heat, Panthers and Marlins turned the Miami area into a full-fledged pro sports town, every little miscue became big news in the highly competitive South Florida media market.

"Part of the reason we got a black eye in reputation was because of the fierce competition on the newspaper beat," said Dalrymple. "There were only two games in town, the Dolphins and the Hurricanes. If you compete for stories, chances are much greater you'll find them. Melvin Bratton walked out of a store with a pair of sunglasses, somebody siphoned gas. Rick Reilly's *Sports Illustrated* story after Vinny's run was really devastating. Our guys were innocently serving up fodder for them.

"It was difficult for Jimmy. He was not condoning things, and nothing happened that was too serious.

"There was the Autogate scandal. The *Miami News* reporters would sit in the parking lot and look at what kind of cars the players were driving and look at license tags and do background checks on the car. In one incident, Alonzo Highsmith was driving a nice car. Both of his parents are professional people and they saved a lot of money for college, and it turned out their son earned a scholarship and they bought him a nice car. He felt he was being profiled.

"There was always a swirl of off-field uneasiness. Even though we were cruising, we couldn't enjoy the 1986 season. Things reached an apex when they wore the fatigues to the Fiesta Bowl and Jerome said to the players at the steak fry, 'That's it, we're out of here.' He felt the Penn State guys had made off-color remarks. When Jerome said, 'We're leaving,' everybody got up and left. Then they lost that game. They had three of the top nine players in the draft on that team, but they let it slip away.

"That was the game that lit the light for the BCS championship game. It was removed from all the New Year's Day games and it was played a day or two after, and it was unopposed on television, with number one versus number two.

"I remember Jimmy went away to coach in the Japan Bowl. I picked him up at the airport when he got back and he still was in a funk.

"As a result, he didn't get the monkey off his back until he beat Oklahoma a year later to win the national title. He loved his time there but grew more fond of his time in Miami after he left.

"After we won the national championship he was accepted by everyone and became as revered almost as much as Howard. When Dennis came in, he had a difficult act to follow. He should be commended for the job he did in making a transition in a situation that was similar. However, he had the luxury of being able to bring in his own staff and start in March rather than early June."

AHEAD OF THE GAME

Rich Dalrymple believed that Bernie Kosar's early exit from the program "was a case study of how his mind is different from others.

"He could see a situation and comprehend the options and execute a winning strategy. He found a way to manipulate the draft so he could pick the team he wanted to play for. Nobody knew anything about a supplemental draft. He and his father had studied it, and Bernie had earned his degree in three years. And if you did that, you could go to the supplemental draft.

"His analytical ability was the reason he was a great leader and championship quarterback. You could see it in his eyes—he had command of the situation. That whole episode was typical of the way he approached things. He was always ahead of the game. When we were starting spring drills in 1985, we had practiced one or two days, and he had to make a decision for the supplemental draft. He didn't go to practice but came out to the field. There was a huge media gathering. He had been out of the loop from commenting, it was all up in the air. People knew Vinny was a helluva talent, but nobody wanted to see Bernie leave. It was the dominant story. I remember after the big media gathering, here was a guy with the weight of the world on his shoulders and the focus of the media. You'd think he'd go to his dorm room and ponder his decision. As I was driving home I saw Bernie and [defensive end] Julio Cortes with their thumbs out, hitchiking down the median of U.S. 1 to go to Key Biscayne to the beach. That son of a gun didn't have a care in the world.

"Almost 20 years later, I was taking my kid to the UM bookstore, and I saw earth being moved and men in hard hats. And there was a sign that said, 'This site under construction as we complete the Bernie Kosar Building.' All I could think of was the tall, skinny kid with the big nose and his thumb sticking out, and now they were putting his name on a building. And he's on the board of trustees."

THE CROSSEYED IBIS

At most colleges, the person inside the costume of a team mascot is a student. That usually has been the case at Miami, too. But there was a notable exception: When the Hurricanes employed a professional mascot, John Routh, from 1984 through the 1992 season. Thanks to the zany and sometimes irreverent escapades of Routh, Sebastian the Ibis became one of the most visible and recognizable mascots in the nation.

He was detained by police and nearly arrested at Florida State, he was shot on Bourbon Street on New Year's Eve in New Orleans, and he punched Florida coach Charley Pell (accidentally, he says).

Routh was also the Miami Maniac, the Hurricane baseball team's mascot, until he became Billy The Marlin of the expansion Florida Marlins. UM baseball coach Ron Fraser, college baseball's premier promoter, hired Routh in 1983 after seeing him perform as South Carolina's mascot, Cocky. Routh also served as assistant director of marketing and promotions.

"My first game as the Ibis was Jimmy Johnson's first game at the Kickoff Classic," Routh said. "I made a major mistake. I was changing in the locker room. It was kind of funny. Jimmy walked in and he looked at me like, 'What are you doing here?' There was no other place to change. Maybe he thought it was tradition, so the rest of my career I changed in the locker room. Mike Short, the equipment manager, said, 'Put your stuff wherever.'"

Routh worked the game in costume the entire first half. What he didn't realize, though, was that since he had rebuilt the costume, he had to change the way he looked through the eyes of the Ibis's head.

"The old costume they'd had since 1980 had a big papier maché head, and the feet were monstrous and it had huge hands," Routh said. "I was used to formalwear gloves like the Maniac wears. I talk with my hands. I made the costume smaller and more comical looking. It was meaner before. I hadn't realized the way it was made. The head had the two eyes, and I made the mistake of focusing out of one eye. In the locker room at the half my eyes were crosseyed. I went to the trainer Kevin O'Neal and said, 'I can't see.' Fortunately I was able to refocus my eyes. I switched looking out of one eye, then the other. Dr. Robert Tanner helped me strengthen my eyes, and I learned how to look out of both."

PUNCHING THE GATORS' COACH

When three touchdowns were scored in the final minute of the Hurricanes' 32-20 victory over Florida at Tampa in 1984, Routh inadvertently ended up in the middle of the wild finish.

"I punched Florida coach Charley Pell in the face on the last play of the game," Routh said. "There was an interception by Tolbert Bain of Miami, and the Florida players gave up and Bain returned it to the end zone. To get to the locker rooms, the teams had to run to opposite sides of the field and crisscross. Bain ran down the sideline, and the Miami guys tackled him in the end zone and jumped on a pile and I was swinging my arms. I hit somebody and a cop grabbed me. I realized, 'Oh, my God, I just punched Charley Pell.' It was totally not intended to happen. The cop grabbed me and I said, 'I'm sorry. I'm sorry.' Pell kept on running to the locker room and realized it was not intentional."

DETAINED AT FSU

When Chief Osceola in Native American clothing charges down onto the field riding an Appaloosa horse named Renegade and plants a flaming spear at midfield to begin a game at Florida State's Doak Campbell Stadium, the crowd invariably goes wild. And sheriffs' deputies in Tallahassee nearly went wild in 1989 when the Ibis acted as if he would douse the flame with a fire extinguisher.

"Many people thought I was arrested," Routh said. "I was detained but never arrested. It took five of them to detain me. This was in the 1989 game when quarterback Craig Erickson got hurt and Gino Torretta was starting. It was one of those things.

"I was thinking, 'What can I do at Florida State?' As the Maniac, I came out on a pony at Mark Light Stadium and put the flame out. They've got their flame and we could put it out. I went to Ed Hudak [one of UM's security officials] and he got me in touch with somebody at the Coral Gables Fire Department and I got a fireman's helmet, a heavy jacket that they wear to fight fires and an air-pressure fire extinguisher, which I still have in my garage.

"I wouldn't have gotten out of Tallahassee alive if I really would have put it out. I wasn't going to get too close to Renegade. But I never had a chance to get on the field. We were in the tunnel, and the way the stands were, they had a chain-link gate and students manned it. I'd gone through this several times knowing students were running this. I was walking in front of Coach Erickson and I heard him say, 'Let's go!' I was there with the fire extinguisher. You could feel the excitement and craziness going. I was holding it sideways and I started charging out to the field, and somebody grabbed me and pulled me back. I was staggered trying to get out of the way of the team. I saw somebody yelling at me and saying, 'Give me the extinguisher!' I squeezed the handle and squirted what turned out to be a Leon County sheriff's deputy.

"The next think I knew five of them had me up against the fence. I found out later one guy threw an elbow to the back of my head. They had one wing behind my back and the other pinned to the fence. Another guy was holding me in the upper chest and neck, and a fourth had the bill and tried to yank the head off. They were literally going crazy. One guy was practically choking me trying to get it off. It ended up pretty ugly. Fans started pelting the cops with cups of ice. Here's five cops beating up on a bird. It looked so silly. To see the look on their faces, you'd think they had caught a murderer.

"I'm yelling, 'Calm down, guys. I'm the mascot from Miami. What are you doing?' Bill Rose, the cheerleading coordinator, came over and kind of calmed the situation down. He said, 'Excuse me, sir, what are you doing to our bird?' The cop said, 'When we tell you to do something, you better do it.' One had his handcuffs out. Another said, 'If you step one foot on the field you're going to jail.' I didn't know what my crime was. The rest of the game I'd look back at the cops and wave and tiptoe one foot on and off the field, toying with them.

"Chief Osceola did his flaming spear thing, and I took the extinguisher and uniform back to the locker room. When the *Miami Herald* printed a picture on Monday and did a story about what happened, I anonymously sent a copy of the story to Bernard Sliger, the FSU president. About two weeks later he sent a letter to Sam saying he wasn't really apologizing, but the cops did their duty protecting the fans of Florida State and Miami. He said, 'What if the mascot scared the horse and he trampled somebody?'

"You've got a guy with a spear and 60,000 fans going crazy and a bird is going to scare him? Sam said it was no big deal. When we went back in 1991, a sheriff's deputy met with me and I was told I was not allowed inside the hash mark when Osceola was doing his thing. What I did was walk back and forth to the hash mark. The team is yelling and screaming at Chief Osceola. That was basically the end of the story. To this day they have someone talk to the Ibis and tell him he can't go near the horse."

"When Jerome Brown was playing at Miami, he said, 'We're going to break the spear.'"

"They didn't, but sometimes they taunted Chief Osceola and Renegade, and sometimes they'd turn their backs and pretend to ignore the scene."

SHOT ON BOURBON STREET

John Routh's last game as the Ibis turned out to be a memorable one long before the kickoff. That was when the Hurricanes met Alabama in the Sugar Bowl at the end of the 1992 season for the national championship.

"I'd already accepted the job to work for the Marlins," Routh said. "I wanted to go out with 30 consecutive victories and two national championships. It was New Year's Eve, and I performed with the cheerleaders at the Hurricane Club party. Around 11:30 we left the hotel on Bourbon Street with the Sunsations cheerleaders. There were 50 to 60 people, boosters, and I was near the back. Harry Rothwell from AllCanes had a bag on his hip, carrying merchandise. I saw two guys point at him and I walked behind him and tapped Harry on the shoulder and said, 'Hold your bag, a couple of guys are watching.' We got to the end of the block and everybody pulled out New Year's Eve horn blowers and somebody started the Miami fight song.

"I turned my head to say something and suddenly there was a stinging, burning sensation on the right side of my face. My first reaction is that somebody hit me with a bottle. I spun around and nobody was within 10 to 15 feet. I never went down, but I was bent over. I wasn't in costume. I was bleeding and one of the Sunsations was screaming. A cop came over and said, 'It looks like we've got our first one.' He said, 'You got shot.' The bullet entered my right temple. It came out of the sky, literally. It was next to my eye. It came under the skin two to three inches and exited the middle of my cheek and grazed my chest. I had a red mark across my chest. An AK 47 bullet was found by a cop right where I was standing. I said, 'What do you mean, I'm your first one?' He said, 'We get 15 to 20 shootings each New Year's Eve. There are two housing projects nearby and what some people do is go up on the roof and shoot bullets toward the French Quarter.' Two nights before that an AP reporter on the 16th floor of his hotel heard a thud and there was a bullet in his chair.

"Connie Nickel [an associate athletic director] waited around with me. We were sitting in the back of the police car and I was holding a towel on my face and assuming they would take me to a hospital. The cop casually asked my name, address, phone number. Connie said, 'Oh, my God. Oh, no, there's [athletic director] Paul Dee and [UM trustee] Ron Stone. They can't see me in the back of the police car.' I said, 'Connie, I'm dying over here.' They took me to the hospital, and I found out two other Miami fans already had been shot.

"They stitched me up and I got to my hotel at 4 a.m. Connie called Ed Hudak, since he was the security director. He was asleep and she said, 'Sorry to wake you, but John Routh got shot.' Ed said, 'Is he alive? Then call me in the morning.'

"I ran into Bob Griese, who was doing the game for ABC. He said, 'You're not going to work, are you?' I got the quote of the week in *Sports Illustrated.* I said, 'It's going to take a lot more than a bullet to the head to keep me out of this game.' I put a bandage on the head of the costume. ABC showed the Ibis on the sideline, splitting the beak. Griese said on TV, 'That's Sebastian. The young guy inside is John Routh and he got shot, but he's a trooper and is out here working the game.'

"I was extremely fortunate. There was very little damage, and you almost can't even tell the scars are there. If it was a half-second earlier or later, it wouldn't have hit me."

SURVIVING NEW ORLEANS

Fleming, the Yamma Yamma Man, recalled that when the Hurricanes traveled to New Orleans for the Sugar Bowl against Alabama in 1993, Dutch Fritzel's German Bar became the Canes' fans' unofficial headquarters.

"He took a liking to the Hurricanes," Fleming said. "We'd do the Not Ready For Prime Time Cheers, such as: 'Beers, beers for old Notre Dame.' And, 'Oooooklahoma! Where they don't know how to throw the ball.'

"We'd go to a pep rally on the balcony of Dutch's place and the street would be full of Canes fans and 'Bama fans. And we'd sing, 'Roll Tide, roll, around the bowl and down the hole, roll Tide roll.' We'd march down the street and we'd be outnumbered. It's unbelievable we survived the trip down Bourbon Street and back."

A SWAT TEAM AND WIDE RIGHT

Here are more John Routh/Ibis tales:
- "Now that students are doing the Ibis, there's more control. I got away with a lot more. I was a professional and they allowed me a little more leeway. Connie Nickel was my advisor and she didn't have a lot of control over me. Coach Fraser taught me that it's a lot easier to apologize than to ask for permission.

"For the Penn State game at the Orange Bowl in 1991, the SWAT team came down in a helicopter. That's against FAA rules in a full stadium. Two guys were dressed as Penn State fans and they hit me over the head with rubber hammers, tied me up and left me on the field. Two drunks came out of the stands and I was yelling, 'Get off the field!' And the helicopter and SWAT team rescued me."

- "Jimmy Johnson was always intense in the locker room. He'd see me and say, 'Go get 'em, John,' or 'Go get 'em,

Sebastian.' Everyone was supportive of the character. It helped build my confidence. I remember at Oklahoma in 1985 when we broke Troy Aikman's leg. It was a cold day, 50 degrees. The Oklahoma people decided not to turn on the hot water in the locker room after we beat them. And Coach was hot about that."

• "In 1984, we were playing Pitt at Homecoming. I came out in a tuxedo, and as I walked out they were doing the captain's thing at midfield for the coin toss. It was a hot Saturday afternoon and we were favored big and the team was not that pumped up. I walked out opposite the referee and [defensive lineman] Kevin Fagan was to my left. The Pitt panther mascot was going to try to trip me. Kevin is a big, tough football player, and he turned from the coin toss and grabbed the inside of the mouth of the panther and pulled him over, slammed him to the ground and yelled, 'Kill him! Kill him!' The panther said through the costume, 'I'm sorry. I'm sorry.'"

• "I had a couple of knee injuries that required surgery. The first happened at the 1990 BYU game when we lost out there. Late in the game they were punting to us. Wesley Carroll [wide receiver] came toward the sideline and tried to jump over a player and he got thrown out of bounds and his foot hit the referee. As Wesley rolled, the BYU equipment guy behind me was trying to get out of the way. I wasn't able to jump, and Wesley slammed right into me and went down. Everybody's attention turned to the referee because he was bleeding. I jumped up on one foot and slapped Wesley on the helmet and went to the bench and yelled for the trainer. I missed two games and rode around on a golf cart with my leg propped up. The next week I drove out like I was still hurt and had a pair of crutches and limped like I was hurt. I smashed the crutches over my knee and went into the C-A-N-E-S routine.

"The other knee injury happened at the Arizona game at the Orange Bowl in 1992. I was underneath the goal post when they missed a field goal at the end of the game and we won 8-7. I saw it miss and ran onto the field. Ryan McNeal [defensive back] was the trail guy. As he came toward me celebrating and we went up to high-five. He's a lot heavier and hit me in the back and I came down with my knee hyperextended backwards. The same left knee I hurt before. Cheerleading itself is a dangerous business, people don't realize it."

• "At the first Wide Right at Tallahassee in 1991, I was underneath the goal post, as nervous as everybody else. I was just to the left of the middle of the goal post. As the kick went up I wasn't positive, but looked at the referee to the left and he looked at the other ref. He had the look like, 'I can't believe he missed this chip shot.' I went out signaling no good before they signaled. Some people thought they made up their mind after they saw me."

Winning with a Swagger

It's Vinny, Not Vinnie

When Vinny Testaverde arrived at Miami in the fall of 1982, nearly everyone spelled his first name "Vinnie." The school listed it that way in press releases and so did the media. Testaverde was too shy to say anything about it until he revealed to the sports information department in 1983 that the name is spelled with a "y" instead of an "ie."

"I didn't want to bother anybody," he said. "Besides, it's still pronounced the same."

Sacked by Hamburgers

Two days before the last regular-season game in 1986 against East Carolina, Testaverde was virtually sacked by a bag of hamburgers. As he drove his red motorscooter on Hurricane Drive after a late-night team meeting at the Hecht Athletic

Center, he looked down at a big bag of hamburgers he was toting and lost control of the scooter, which hit a curb. He suffered extensive abrasions on the left side of his body but no broken bones or torn muscles.

"Vinny doesn't own a car," said coach Jimmy Johnson, who was in his car behind Testaverde when his franchise quarterback tumbled into the curb. "His dad and I both frowned at this motor scooter thing, but he assured us he only drove it on campus, so ... "

Testaverde watched from the sideline as senior Geoff Torretta (older brother of Gino) threw three touchdown passes to lead Miami past East Carolina 36-10.

After the game, Testaverde's No. 14 jersey was retired. A few days later he won the Heisman Trophy. Two days later he visited the White House and president Ronald Reagan.

He had only 10 practices before the Fiesta Bowl game against Penn State for the national championship. He still had scabs and wasn't 100 percent when the team arrived in Phoenix. He was intercepted five times, including the final seconds in the end zone in the 14-10 loss. It had been 47 days since his last game, and it showed against the second-ranked Nittany Lions. UM amassed 445 yards and allowed 162, but receivers dropped five passes.

"The rustiness of the quarterback, the focal point of our offense, cost us," said Johnson. "I don't blame Vinny. It was a freak accident. Looking back, the backup quarterback (Geoff Torretta) might have given us a chance to win the national championship because he had been at practice. We had been so dominating, the only way we would lose it was to beat ourselves."

SUPERMAN AND PIZZAS

Vinny Testaverde may have clinched the Heisman Trophy on a wild, zigzag scramble that became known as "The Play." It happened in the middle of the second quarter when Miami, ranked second, was host to top-ranked Oklahoma in the Orange Bowl at midseason in 1986.

As Testaverde dropped back to pass from the Sooners' 34-yard line, he was flushed out of the pocket. He scrambled to the right sideline about 10 yards behind the line of scrimmage. A defender tried to stop him but managed only to make Testaverde's left shoulder pad flap out from under his jersey.

Testaverde then ran toward the left sideline and stiff-armed a defender before being forced out of bounds after gaining 10 yards.

"The man has an 'S' on his chest," said Oklahoma's All-America linebacker Brian Bosworth.

"Seldom do you win a Heisman on a single game," recalled Rich Dalrymple, who was Miami's sports information director. "I still maintain Vinny won it on a very impressive body of work, but he put it on ice with that one scramble. It was a big game, number one versus two, Vinny and his candidacy versus Brian Bosworth, who with all the hype and intrigue made a legitimate run to be the first defender to win the Heisman. It was an old, traditional power versus the new, up-and-coming power. It was all there and was on CBS. Because of the buildup, it seemed like the moment was there for somebody to make a statement, and Vinny made it. It seemed like that play lasted about two minutes. When it was over his helmet was twisted cockeyed, and Brent Musberger was left speechless. It was the type of play that left you breathless, and it took the air out of Oklahoma. That one, single play is what cemented the Heisman. After that the race was over."

Soon after "The Play," it seemed as if every media person in the nation wanted to talk with Testaverde. Cincinnati radio talk show host Bill Cunningham tracked him down the night before a game at Cincinnati. Cunningham offered the Hurricanes 20 pizzas if they could get Testaverde on the phone. Vinny talked and Cunningham delivered.

"On Friday nights, we have a segment on the show where we talk about embarrassing moments in lovemaking," Cunningham said. "Miami's kicker, Greg Cox, called the show and said some of the players were listening to the show and cracking up.

"I said I wanted to talk to Vinny and that we had a tie-in with a pizza parlor and would deliver 20 pizzas if he'd get him on the phone. Ten minutes later, Vinny was on the line.

"I asked him if there were girls there and the team was having a good time, and he said, 'Oh, no, sir, we're having meetings with the coaches.' I asked if they were watching X-rated movies and he said, 'Oh, no, sir, we're studying offensive schemes.' Every time I jabbed, he counterpunched in Boy Scout fashion."

THE WRONG BUS

NFL draft day in 1987 turned out to be an unprecedented bonanza for the Miami program as three players were among the first nine selected. Vinny Testaverde was the top pick (by Tampa Bay), running back Alonzo Highsmith was third (by Houston) and the ninth was defensive tackle Jerome Brown (by Philadelphia). Highsmith contributed as a backup freshman fullback on the 1983 national championship team and started thereafter.

"Probably one of the funniest stories about Jimmy Johnson happened his first year there in 1984," Highsmith said. "He didn't know that one of the busses that took us to the games was full of guys like Jerome Brown and me, guys who joked around a lot. The other bus was more laid back. Coach Johnson was used to nobody saying a word on the bus. He didn't realize he had gotten on the wrong bus, the noisy one. We were joking and laughing. Father Leo was in the back, and Coach kept look-ing back and wanted to yell at us. But it was the priest who was telling all the jokes. After that, Coach split the busses up into offense and defense."

THE ROAD WARRIORS

The Hurricanes lost only two road games in five seasons under Jimmy Johnson. And that tradition of success away from Miami covered more than two decades. The Hurricanes constructed the best road record (not including neutral sites) in the nation from 1983-2004, going 88-20 for a winning percent-age of .821.

Alonzo Highsmith believes one factor in starting that road success was the brashness of the team.

"I remember the time we went to Oklahoma in 1985 and Coach Johnson had never beaten them before while he was at Oklahoma State," Highsmith said. "All the coaches Jimmy brought with him from Oklahoma State were kind of nervous and uptight. But here we are, Melvin Bratton is yelling on the bus, opening the window and yelling to the fans.

"After that game [which Miami won 27-14] Coach Johnson realized this was a special group of guys and they are not intimidated and they enjoy playing on the road."

Players and coaches say the main reason for the team's suc-cess on the road was that they treated it as a business trip.

"Coach Johnson really stressed the road," Highsmith said. "It got to the point where it was all business mentality-wise. There were specific techniques to winning on the road. But there were no visiting families and friends. It was all about foot-ball. He would say, 'I don't want to meet your families. I can do that after the season.'

"We used to love going into other teams' stadiums. It was a natural high. We relished the moment. There's nothing better

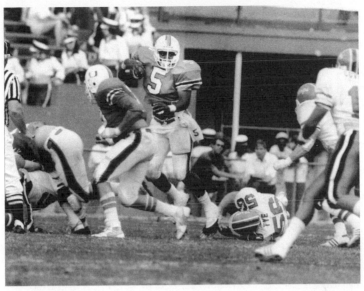

Melvin Bratton

than to spoil their evening and day. The only time I saw Miami intimidated on the road was the Sugar Bowl at the end of the 1985 season. There were 72,000 voices against us." And they sang "Rocky Top" seemingly a zillion times as Tennessee won, 35-7.

Steve Walsh, who quarterbacked the 1987 national champions, believes the Hurricanes played well on the road "because we were so confident in our ability. We viewed a hostile environment as a chance to prove to the fans that we were truly better than they were. Offensive coordinator Gary Stevens always would say to us, 'They're coming to see us. Put on a show!'"

THRIVING IN HOSTILE ENVIRONMENTS

Rich Dalrymple, former sports information director, believed Johnson's teams "were successful at playing well on road, and maybe playing better, because they thrived in a hostile environment. In 1987 they went to Arkansas, which hadn't lost in Little Rock in 10 years and had a good team. Jim Brock, chairman of the Cotton Bowl, was there, and he had his hands in his face at halftime when Miami led, 31-0. He said, "That's the most devastating half of football I've seen in my life." The game had special significance for Jimmy because he was passed over for Lou Holtz. They took care of business.

"I remember a game in 1988, LSU was going to be SEC champion, and it was a Saturday night on ESPN. Mike Archer, a former Miami player and assistant coach, was the head coach, and Baton Rouge was a very difficult place to play and there was a driving rainstorm. I thought our passing game would be hindered, but the final score was 44-3," Dalrymple said.

"At some point during all these huge road victories, someone asked Bratton why the Hurricanes played well on the road. He said, 'I don't know. I think we like to go into people's backyards and turn over the garbage cans.'

"They had a big victory at Oklahoma, 27-14, in 1985 when the Sooners were ranked third. John McVeigh and Jerome Brown sacked Troy Aikman and broke his leg. They had a big victory at Gainesville in 1986, 23-15, in one of the biggest slugfests I've ever seen.

"Jerome was the heart and soul of that attitude, and that attitude started under Howard Schnellenberger. He understood that the type of kids they had thrived on emotion and let them go. And Jimmy said they had a special thing going and built upon it. It was very intimidating and awe-inspiring at times when they would take a quality opponent and tear them apart."

Michael Irvin

Spirited Play, Work Ethic

Highsmith believes that "another thing that made the program unique was the spirit the team played with. We were the team that wasn't supposed to be. Everyone took that with a chip on their shoulder.

"Our freshman year in 1983 we started with that cocky, arrogant this-is-our-stadium attitude. Tony Fitzpatrick, Fred Robinson and all those guys started it and we carried it over—talking crap, pointing fingers and high-fiving. I think a lot of teams respected that. Guys would come up and say, 'Our coaches won't let us do that, and we wish they did.'

"But the thing I remember most is the work ethic we had under Coach Johnson and Coach Schnellenberger. I remember when Schnellenberger left, we were a little happy because he made us work so hard. Then Coach Johnson picked it up more.

"This team was very dependent on each other. Players challenged each other every day. We didn't accept guys quitting. If you had thin skin, you couldn't play for Miami.

"We'd take offense when a top player would come in. If you were supposed to be the top guy coming in as a freshman, you were going to get challenged the first day on the field. If you played defense you had to go up against Brett Perriman, Michael Irvin and Brian Blades every day. Irvin on his first day as a freshmen got into a fight with some offensive linemen."

TALENT AND TALK

On the 1986 team that was filled with big-time talkers, defensive tackle Dan Sileo was one of the best at tackling and talking. He's still talking as a radio sports show host in Florida.

He says he was the creator of wearing fatigues to games (Tony Fitzpatrick, circa 1983, will contest that), and he believes the '86 Hurricanes were the all-time best and biggest under-achievers in college football history.

"We had so many great players," Sileo said. "Jimmy Johnson lined us up [at a reunion] and looked at the staff and players and said, 'Maybe this is the greatest Pro Bowl team I've ever seen.'

"We had Michael Irvin and Russell Maryland was just a young pup. And the coaching staff included Dave Wannstedt and Gary Stevens and Butch Davis and Tony Wise. And Dave Campo and Tommy Tuberville were graduate assistants. Jimmy said, 'When you wore the UM colors you were so proud, you took so much pride.'

"I remember going up to Pitt. Jimmy never liked a lot of b.s. on trips. Alonzo Highsmith said something and cracked a joke. Jimmy ran over with his hair flying and yelled at this walk-on nobody guy, 'If I catch you talking again, I'll put you back on a plane.'

"I was the creator of the fatigues, when we played Oklahoma at the Orange Bowl in 1986. Jerome Brown took it to a new level for the Fiesta Bowl. I showed up at the Oklahoma game in fatigues. I always did that for home games. Jerome said to me, 'Can't your family afford clothes?' I was getting ready for battle.

"The greatest game I saw was the 1985 game at Oklahoma with Jerome. He had 20 tackles, a sack, a fumble recovery and an interception, and he broke Troy Aikman's leg. He dismantled that team.

"The greatest spectacle was that Fiesta Bowl against Penn State. There was so much hype around it. I covered the Rose Bowl when Miami beat Nebraska but there was no energy like the Fiesta Bowl. That was like a Super Bowl, with 400 media people.

"I still believe the 1986 Miami team was the greatest college football team and the most underachieving. If we had won, it would have gone down as the greatest ever. We had three timeouts left in that last drive when we were behind 14-10. On the sidelines I looked over at Jerome Brown when we got to the 10, and we didn't want to watch the plays. We knew he [Vinny Testaverde] was going to throw a pick. He threw one, and we all looked at each other and had go back on the field. It ended so crazy.

"At the steak fry [a few days before the game], Jerome said, 'Sileo, let's get up there on the stage.' I didn't want to fry anybody. He got up there and screwed the whole thing up. One of our players said, 'Did the Japanese sit down with the Americans before Pearl Harbor?' It became a good versus evil thing, it was a hated game. Rick Reilly fueled it from *Sports Illustrated*. They had the media fueling Miami as us being the bad guys. That followed us the next couple of years, the media tagged us with that. Reilly called me the Mouth of the South."

WELL, RUN SOMETHING

More tales from Dan Sileo:

• On Butch Davis, his defensive line coach at Miami: "I love him to death and we talk all time. He always had a big Arkansas twang and he'd say, 'You got to get down in that stance and be like a scalded ape. Come down on that line like a scalded ape.'

"Jimmy Jones [defensive line teammate of Sileo's] almost drowned in Butch's canal. Butch had a party for his defensive line, like Tony Wise would have for the offensive line and Dave Campo would have for the defensive backs. Jones got some beer and he couldn't drink and couldn't swim. It was a pool party, and for some crazy reason he jumped in the canal and got out to the middle. I said, 'Jerome, he's drowning.' He went under and we had to dive in and save him. He was barely breathing. He was just having a good time and got caught up."

• On Jimmy Johnson: "I never thought Jimmy was a great Xs and Os guy. In 1985 we played Louisville and it was the first time Howard came back to the Orange Bowl. We were standing there at the end of the game and we were killing them 45-7. And Jimmy looked over at [offensive coordinator] Gary Stevens and said, 'Run that halfback option.' Gary said, 'We don't have an option.' And Jimmy said, 'Well, run something.'"

MICHAEL VERSUS DEION

On October 3, 1987, at Tallahassee, Miami was ranked third and FSU fourth, and many felt it was FSU's best team to date. The Seminoles appeared en route to a rout as they led 19-3 late in the third quarter. That's when FSU cornerback Deion "Neon" Sanders came up to wide receiver Michael Irvin and said, "Michael, you might as well quit running so hard and blocking so hard, 'cause it's all over for today. Take it easy, Mike, don't hurt yourself."

Irvin replied: "Oh, no. We play Hurricane football all day. We're going to keep balling [playing] all day."

Irvin and Miami backed those words with perhaps the greatest comeback to date. Steve Walsh threw a 49-yard touchdown pass to Melvin Bratton and threw for two points to Brian Blades to make it 19-11 with 1:49 left in the third quarter.

Early in the fourth Walsh hit Irvin for 26 yards and a touchdown, then passed to Warren Williams for two more points and a 19-19 tie. End Dan Stubbs set up the touchdown with an interception.

FSU mounted a drive, but Bennie Blades recovered a fumbled snap by quarterback Danny McManus at UM's 17. Four plays later, Walsh hit Irvin down the right sideline for 73 yards and a touchdown, and Greg Cox's extra point made it 26-19 with 2:22 left.

FSU scored with 42 seconds left to make it 26-25. Coach Bobby Bowden elected to go for two points, but the McManus pass for tight end Pat Carter was batted down by cornerback Bubba McDowell.

UM was outgained 426-306 yards, and FSU kicker Derek Schmidt missed two field goals and an extra point.

"If I had to do it over, I'd kick it for the tie," Bowden said.

Both teams went unbeaten the rest of the year as the Hurricanes won the national title and FSU finished second in the final polls.

Rich Dalrymple, former sports information director, said that was "Walsh's coming-of-age game right there. He was a smart guy, he won't turn it over. He didn't have a great arm and physical tools, but he made some tremendous throws and rallied them.

"After Bubba knocked down that pass, there was a hush over that place like you've never seen. Sebastian the Ibis held up a sign that said 'STATE CHAMPIONS.' And on that day we knew if we'd win, that we were on our way to winning the national championship."

God Felt Sorry

The Hurricanes went into the 1987 season having to replace seven players taken in the NFL draft, including the three first-round picks—Testaverde, Highsmith and Brown. Yet the 1987 team, which opened the season ranked 10th, went undefeated and won Miami's second national championship.

Why did the talent-loaded 1986 team come up short and the reloading team of 1987 win it all?

"I think it was just destiny," said wide receiver Michael Irvin, who played on both teams. "The 1986 team was better. In '86 we outplayed Penn State. We had a much better team, we just weren't due to win the game.

"It was just like in 1987 when Florida State outplayed us but we won the game 26-25. It had to be destiny. God felt sorry for us. He said, 'These guys have been working hard for a few years. Let's give them a championship.'"

The 31 Season

The Hurricanes came within one play, a highly controversial one, of going undefeated in 1988 and winning back-to-back national championships. Call it the "31 Season."

In the opener they stunned Florida State, 31-0. In the second game at Michigan they overcame a 30-14 deficit to win 31-30. And in the fifth game at Notre Dame they lost 31-30 on a call that still riles up Canes followers.

Miami opened the defense of its championship at home but was ranked sixth, and the visiting Seminoles were number one and featured Heisman Trophy candidate Sammie Smith at tailback. Five Hurricane ball carriers outgained him as he was limited to six yards in 10 carries. The Canes intercepted five passes and handed FSU its first shutout since 1976. It was the sixth consecutive season Miami had defeated the preseason top-ranked team.

What riled up the Hurricanes? Perhaps because they were underdogs at home. Or maybe it was the cocky rap video the Seminoles recorded that summer.

Jimmy Johnson didn't give a fiery speech before this game. He simply called the entire team into the office, popped in the rap video and walked out of the room.

Two weeks later at Michigan the Hurricanes returned to Ann Arbor, Michigan, site of Johnson's only road loss so far at Miami. Michigan led 30-14 midway through the third quarter. Fans were chanting, "Na na na na, hey hey hey, goodbye." Hurricanes radio announcer Sonny Hirsch declared the 32-game regular-season winning streak was over, and an ABC announcer said Miami had lost.

But the Hurricanes scored 17 points in the final five and a half minutes to win in front of 105,834 at the Big House.

"Everyone kept their cool," said quarterback Steve Walsh. "No one was running around like a Chinese fire drill. Hopefully, my personality had something to do with that, though I think I got a couple more gray hairs."

Father Leo Armbrust, the Hurricanes' team chaplain and a confidante to many players and coaches, related this story about the Michigan game: "Few people knew that the week before the game, assistant coaches Art Kehoe and Gary Stevens were going through some old plays in the playbook and throwing some out and keeping some. Art would say, 'Gary, what about this one?' And Gary would look at some of it, and if it was worth keeping he would put it in this week. In the press box in the fourth quarter, they knew they had nothing to lose. Some of those plays Gary thought of discarding, he started to put them in and ran a two-minute offense. And Walsh had a field day in the second half, and Cleveland Gary, Dale Dawkins and Rob Chudzinski had classic games."

Then at South Bend, T-shirt sales were brisk as bitterness toward Miami reached a crescendo. "Catholics vs. Convicts" and "Even God Hates Miami" were popular shirts. UM had seven turnovers and there was a controversial call on a fumble by Gary at the Notre Dame one in the fourth quarter. Moments later Walsh threw an 11-yard TD pass to Andre Brown with 45 seconds left, but his conversion pass to halfback Leonard Conley was broken up. The teams went unbeaten the rest of the way as Notre Dame won the national title and Miami finished number two.

"About a week or so after that Notre Dame game," said Rich Dalrymple, "Richard Nixon sent Jimmy a letter and said, 'I watched the game, and I think you guys got the short end of the stick on officiating. Whether it was a fumble or a first down, you got took.' Jimmy showed me the letter. He said, 'There's a guy that knows something about things going against you.'"

THE DANCING BEAR

The first time Russell Maryland played football, he hated it. But he went on to become the best defensive lineman in college football.

His introduction to football came when he was around nine years old and he woke up one day to find that his father had put football gear in his bed and his brother's bed.

"We weren't thrilled," Maryland said. "We just wanted to go ride our bicycles. But our father made us suit up and go to a nearby park and block each other. I hated it. I didn't get any happier when he made us run the eight blocks home."

His father forced him to play high school football to teach him discipline. Maryland grew to 321 pounds as a senior lineman at Chicago's Whitney Young High School. The only schools offering scholarships were Indiana and Miami, which decided to take a long shot on "the fat kid with the quick feet." He received Miami's last scholarship in 1986, lost 50 pounds before playing as a redshirt freshman in 1987 and finished his

Russell Maryland

Miami career in 1990 as a consensus first-team All-American and the school's first winner of the Outland Trophy.

Teammates called him "the dancing bear" because, as defensive end Greg Mark said, "he's always jumping over and around people like he's dancing." They also called him "The Conscience" because he was a low-key leader who wasn't big on taunting and flaunting.

He was the first player chosen in the 1991 NFL draft, picked by Jimmy Johnson's Dallas Cowboys.

PARTING WORDS

Yes, there was a soft side to Jimmy Johnson.

"The day he left Miami for the Dallas Cowboys was the only time I saw him cry," said Rich Dalrymple. "He had a very short speech, and the last thing he said was, 'You know the job you have to do. Players win championships, not coaches.' He was in tears. He started to walk out, then he turned around and said, 'And one more thing. You get after Notre Dame's tail.' And he walked out the door."

CHAPTER 9

Home, Sweet Home

THE X FACTOR

Many college football fans wonder how the University of Miami managed to win five national championships under four different head coaches in less than two decades. It's not just about the coaches. It's about the players, as UM trustee Ron Stone found out in chatting with Dennis Erickson and his staff just before they won their second national title in three years.

"We were sitting up in Dennis's suite in Sheraton Bal Harbour for the 1991 national championship game in the Orange Bowl," said Stone. "We house there. I was there with a bunch of coaches one day after practice, and we were in a general conversation about what it was like for them to take over the program and the success they'd had.

"I was complimenting Dennis on maintaining the focus and intensity of the program. Dennis started chuckling. He said, 'You don't understand what we didn't understand. It's not us. We say this place has got something no place else in the U.S. has or ever had. It's what we call the X factor. Right, guys?'"

Dennis Erickson

"Yes, Coach," the assistants replied.

"What's the X factor?" said Stone.

"It's the ex-player factor," said Erickson.

"You mean the connection the football alumni maintain with the players?"

"Yes. People don't understand. The ex-players are on the phone with players who took over their positions, talking and encouraging them for the next opponent. It's an unbelievable thing for us as coaches. Usually the biggest thing for us to focus on is the psychological factor and edge at game time. But at this program we don't have to do any of that. The ex-players do, and we can work on game plans and put them in the best position on the field so they can use the ex-factor."

HURRICANE ANDREW

The Hurricanes approached the 1992 season with a goal to "win one for the thumb," a fifth national championship ring. On August 24, two weeks before the opening game at Iowa, one of the fiercest storms ever recorded slammed into the southern tip of the state. Hurricane Andrew, labeled the most devastating natural disaster in U.S. history, destroyed 650,000 homes and left 250,000 people homeless. The homes of several players and coaches, including head coach Dennis Erickson, defensive coordinator Sonny Lubick and star linebacker Michael Barrow, were severely damaged. Erickson and his family rode out the storm in the closet of assistant coach Rich Olson.

The UM campus was on the north edge of the worst destruction and had to be closed because there was no electricity or water. UM officials decided to move practice 140 miles north to Vero Beach's Dodgertown, spring training home of the Los Angeles Dodgers.

In an emotional game dedicated to South Florida residents, the Hurricanes defeated Iowa 24-7 behind a solid defense and the passing of Gino Torretta.

"This wasn't just a game," said defensive end Rusty Medearis. "This was a statement to the people of South Florida. We wanted them to know that if we can overcome, so can the city. And it can be better than it ever has."

Added Erickson: "This has been about as tough as anyone could go through. We had personal tragedies, a tragedy that affects a whole community. I hope I never have to go through something like that again. I knew they would come out and play hard because they have a great deal of pride. ... They were focused and were being a part of Hurricane football. They realize how important Hurricane football is to South Florida. We got letter after letter from people who said, 'Don't worry about us.' People without homes were trying to find a place to watch the game on TV."

FAMILY BUSINESS: WRESTLING

Dwayne Johnson contributed to the Hurricanes' success in the early 1990s as a defensive lineman, but he had the misfortune of being at Miami at the same time as Warren Sapp (1992-94).

Ron Stone, longtime board of trustees member, watched games in those days from the sidelines and remembers talking to Johnson often. Little did Stone or members of the Hurricane family imagine what the future would hold for Johnson, that he would go on to become the mega-star The Rock in professional wrestling and the movies. Stone recalled their conversation on the last home game of Johnson's senior year.

"He and I used to stand on the sideline during games and chat about the game," Stone said. "All the seniors had been introduced during the pregame. During the game we were on the sidelines in our usual standing spot at the right end of the players area."

Stone turned to Johnson and said, "So Dwayne, what kind of plans have you got after this? You going to try to get on with somebody, get drafted?"

"There's no way I'm going to be drafted," Johnson replied. "I don't think I'll try to play pro football. This has been absolutely fantastic, the greatest thing I could imagine. But I need to move on with my life. This part is over."

"So what does that mean? What are you thinking of doing?"

"I'll probably go into the family business."

"What kind of business is your family in?"

"The wrestling business."

"Wrestling business? Like WWF type?"

"Yes. Exactly."

"What do they do, promote events?"

"No, they're wrestlers. My father and three uncles. It's in the family blood."

"Are you telling me you're going to be a wrestler in the ring?"

"Yeah, I think I'm going to try it."

"Well, good luck. I hope it works out for you."

When the game was over, Stone said, "Good luck with your wrestling." He never saw him again.

"I don't exactly follow WWF," said Stone. "Then one day about 1998 or '99 my wife says, 'Do you know this guy your son is crazy about—The Rock?' I said, 'Who's that?' She said, 'He's the new superstar of TV wrestling. I heard he used to play for UM.' I said, 'What's his name?' I thought, it couldn't be. I went to the internet and called up WWF and put in The Rock. Undeniably, there he was in the family business. I saw him on television, and it was fantastic."

FROM RAW TO ROCK

Dwayne Johnson was a latecomer to football, playing only two seasons in high school in Bethlehem, Pennsylvania. After his redshirt season at Miami in 1990, he started just one game in four years for the Hurricanes.

That wasn't because of a lack of talent. He obviously could have started for many teams. While at Miami, Johnson underwent shoulder surgery twice, and his senior year he had two ruptured discs in his back. Moreover, the Hurricanes were loaded with stars at defensive tackle—first-round draft choices Russell Maryland and Warren Sapp and second-rounder Pat Riley.

Art Kehoe, the Miami assistant coach who recruited Johnson, said, "When I went through Pennsylvania in the springtime, the coaches said, 'You need to check this kid out. He's kind of wild, but he's an immense, fast athletic dude. He's real flexible, a raw guy who hasn't played a lot. Bob Karmelowicz [defensive line coach] kind of took him over, but I did the school and home visits.

"The day I signed quarterback Frank Costa—you could sign them on the road then, they didn't FedEx it—Bob said when he went into his house, his dad, Rocky, and his uncles, all Samoans, were all in the house. They were all drinking saki and jumping up and down and screaming their little baby was playing for the Miami Hurricanes. It was hilarious. Bob called me at Costa's to interrupt us and said, 'I want to let you know I got a kid who's going to be sacking your kid's butt.'

"Dwayne wanted to play at Miami. He did a good job. He had a couple of injuries and just lacked experience."

Karmelowicz said Johnson "worked harder than anybody and was a good college player."

Greg Mark, Miami's defensive line coach who was a graduate assistant when Johnson was a senior, added: "Dwayne was a very articulate young man. He had a fire about him. He was a competitor. As far as personality and what he portrayed as The Rock, that's not Dwayne. It's surprising at times to see him act that way, but it's fun for him. Countless times I've watched interviews with famous actors saying it's so much more fun being a villain. He's becoming an action hero, not so much villain. His character in wrestling was as the people's champion, and he gets to play the thug a little bit. You could see his flamboyance and competitiveness on the field at Miami."

Johnson came from the same home town as former Hurricane Ed Hudak, who for years has been part of UM's football security, Bethlehem, Pennsylvania, and Hudak got to know Johnson's family.

"The Rock was very low key," Hudak said. "My dad said, 'Look at this kid from Freedom High School. He has only been playing football for two years, he's a big lifter and looks like he has great ability.' We hit it off. He was quiet and soft spoken, and you could tell he was a great athlete.

"I remember one time I was going home and I said to him, 'Do you want me to pick up anything from your house?' He said, 'I need a boom box and some other stuff.' I met his mom and dad and said, 'We're taking care of your son.' Obviously I'm

Dwayne Johnson

not up on Samoan culture. She says, 'Could you take your shoes off?' They're a sweet family. The work ethic he had in the weight room, I could see where it came from. They're a close family. It was almost a natural assumption that he'd make it on either side, football or wrestling. His acting has really improved. At Miami he was always one of the guys. They called him Dewey."

Johnson wasn't the first former Hurricane football player to go on to pro wrestling fame. So did Larry Pfohl, who became Lex Lugar on the wrestling circuit. He was a starting offensive guard for Lou Saban in 1978, but his Miami career was abruptly ended when Saban dismissed him from the team because of damage he caused to his apartment and to an Atlanta hotel room.

THIRD AND 44

In Dennis Erickson's first season, 1989, Miami lost at FSU 28-10 when freshman Gino Torretta had to fill in for injured Craig Erickson and was intercepted four times, and the offense was stopped at the FSU one three times.

That turned out to be the lone defeat of the season. The Hurricanes moved back into national title contention against top-ranked and defending champion Notre Dame at the Orange Bowl before 81,634, the largest regular-season home crowd ever. The Hurricanes won 27-10, snapping Notre Dame's 23-game winning streak. It was the sixth time the defense didn't allow a touchdown that season.

The defining moments of the game and the season came in a 22-play, 80-yard drive that lasted 10 minutes and 47 seconds. A personal foul penalty, a sack of Craig Erickson and a fumble that center Bobby Garcia recovered at the Miami three put the Hurricanes into a third down-and-44 situation.

No problem. Erickson threw deep to wide receiver Randal Hill for 44 yards and a first down, and Miami eventually scored on a five-yard pass to Dale Dawkins.

"That was one of Miami's most impressive victories," said former sports information director Rich Dalrymple. "It was no contest. That was the peak of the Notre Dame-Miami rivalry and the hostility and dislike for each other. That was our home game after we felt we didn't get a fair shake at South Bend the previous year. Converting third and 44 with Craig Erickson hitting Randal Hill sticks out in my mind. That was pure Hurricane arrogance and attitude. Then we lost the next year in South Bend. The feelings of disdain weren't good for the series to continue, and it's a shame it didn't."

T-Shirt Inspiration

Geoff Torretta served as the backup to Vinny Testaverde and made his first trip to New York's Downtown Athletic Club in 1986 to accompany Testaverde to the Heisman Trophy award ceremony. While there, Torretta bought a Downtown Athletic Club sweatshirt with the Heisman Trophy insignia on it. He took it home to Pinole, California, and gave it to his brother Gino, then 17.

One day their mother, Connie, asked Gino why he wore the shirt so often, and he jokingly replied, "I'm going to win that thing. You watch."

He did in 1992, becoming the second Hurricane player to win college football's premier award.

The Streak

A large sign on the north side of the upper deck at the Orange Bowl said: "THE CITY OF MIAMI WEL-COMES YOU TO THE ORANGE BOWL."

It could have said: "WELCOME TO COLLEGE FOOT-BALL'S HOUSE OF HORRORS," because that's where the Hurricanes went unbeaten for nearly a decade, from October 12, 1985, until Washington ended it on September 24, 1994. The 58-game winning streak broke the record of 57 home victories set by Alabama at Bryant-Denny Stadium in Tuscaloosa, Ala.

Players and coaches say it's the atmosphere and the fans that made the Orange Bowl special.

"It's about as tough and intense an atmosphere as I've ever had to take a team," said Notre Dame's Lou Holtz. The Irish were outscored 109-17 in losing three games during the streak.

Three other top-ranked teams fell: Oklahoma 28-16 in 1986; Oklahoma 20-14 in the 1988 Orange Bowl Classic; and Florida State 31-0 in 1988.

"It's the atmosphere, the smoke, the ghosts of those who played there before," said Miami wide receiver Chris T. Jones. "It's a feeling that's so unbelievable, and the crowd is so into the game. It goes back to when the Dolphins played there."

Running back Melvin Bratton added: "As a player, you are so pumped up you could run through a brick wall." Wide receiver Horace Copeland added: "I'm scared to play there, and it's our home crowd. It's very intimidating. It's worse at night, because it's dark and kind of spooky inside."

COUNTRY BUMPKIN TO PRO BOWL

Greg Mark, the Hurricanes' defensive line coach from 1996 to 2005, played alongside Cortez Kennedy on the highly talented defensive line at Miami in 1988 and 1989. And he was a graduate assistant during Warren Sapp's reign of terror as a defensive tackle at Miami from 1992-94. Mark recalled that Sapp, who won the Lombardi Award as the nation's top lineman in 1994, was so dominant in practice that many times they'd have to take him out so the offense could move the ball past the line of scrimmage.

"I remember," Mark said, "that Dennis Erickson in the middle of a spring scrimmage or practice would say to me, 'I'll give you the signal to get him out of there so we can run the offense, or at least get the ball off once or twice.' Warren was such a dominant figure. On the positive side, he made our offense that much better. They knew it and he knew it. And he'd tell them he knew it." Mark on Kennedy: "When he came in he was just a country bumpkin from Arkansas. During two-a-days when he first came in, he was extremely out of shape. He came from a junior college, and his whole goal in life was to become

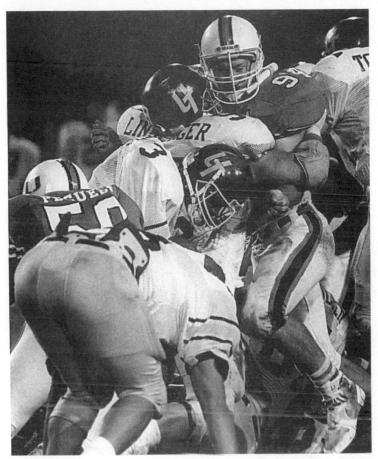

Greg Mark

a state trooper. We were out running and he was dying and falling over. He said, 'The heck with this. I'm going back to Arkansas and be a state trooper.'

"He came from a small town and came to Miami and got around the team we had and the work ethic we had, and he ended up becoming a role model that younger guys would look up to. He has tremendous character. He went from being an overweight JC defensive lineman who wanted to be a state trooper to being a 10- or 11-year NFL veteran who made Pro Bowls."

Both Sapp and Kennedy were on the sideline of the Hurricanes' victory over Florida in the 2001 Sugar Bowl "and they were going at each other," Mark said. "Warren said to Cortez, 'You make Pro Bowl this year?' He was busting his chops that he didn't and said, 'How many times did you actually make Pro Bowl yet?' What shut it all up was when Cortez said, 'How many All-Century teams did you make?'"

A CLONE OF JEROME

The youngest of six children, Warren Sapp wasn't allowed to play youth-league football in the tiny central Florida town of Plymouth, because his mother, Annie, thought it was too dangerous.

"I'll be careful," Warren said.

Eventually he played and became a highly recruited star as a linebacker, tight end and punter at Apopka High School. When he gained 40 pounds during his redshirt season at Miami, coaches began to think of him as an intimidating lineman.

"They asked me to try it," Sapp said. "I waited around about three days and I talked to some people. They said, 'Well, you've got good feet and you look like you can play. Give it a shot.' So I did that and I got to liking it. It became fun."

He was the starter in 1993 and 1994. Tommy Tuberville, the defensive coordinator, called him "an exact clone of Jerome Brown. His personality. His athletic skills. His build. He's a perfect replica of a defensive tackle in college football. And he's a hard worker."

Warren Sapp

He was a consensus All-American in 1994, the first Miami player to win the Lombardi Award, and was one of six finalists invited to the Heisman Trophy presentation.

He made a lasting impression of Florida State's Bobby Bowden, who said, "Sapp ought to be illegal."

Family Affair

Father Leo Armbrust, the Hurricanes' team chaplain from the Schnellenberger through the Erickson eras, has been as close to the program as anyone. He tended to their spiritual needs and consoled them after the deaths of several players, including Jerome Brown, and the murders of Shane Curry and Marlin Barnes.

"I think the most important feature of the success revolved around the tradition they began to establish in viewing themselves as a family. And that is often misunderstood. People who live down the block and only see a family externally make judgements. What kept things together was the feeling of unity. Howard started something, Jimmy improved upon it certainly, Dennis inherited that as Butch did. The most amazing thing is that Miami has changed athletic directors and football coaches and the program keeps on winning. Is it in the water?

"Michigan State, Michigan, Notre Dame, some of these programs have incredible traditions, but the one thing that stands out at Miami is family. And the sense of family will beat tradition every day of the week. It's most demonstrated by the fact that so many who played there coached there. There has been stability and permanency that you need in any family.

"A great thing the university continues to do is bring guys back the night before the spring game for a reunion. And Jimmy has gone to that this year. That says a lot about what that program continues to do in shaping these young men."

Larry Coker believed in the importance of the reunion. "Each year we try to have former players back to watch practice and have a dinner and get a chance to reunite," he said. "Also the young players get to meet some of the old guys. It's a great event. In the spring of 2004, we had our largest ever, a total of 230 players. Some were recent graduates and some were distant graduates.

"They have a great social time. And I'm sure the tales do get better as the years go on. They have lots of arguments about which team was better at Miami."

And when the reunions are held, the current players recognize many of the former players because so many of them have been highly visible in the NFL.

"We have so many recognizable players," Coker said. "When I was at Ohio State, current players didn't know who Hopalong Cassidy is. But there are so many of players here who are still recognizable. When I came here in 1995, all these former quarterbacks except George Mira were still playing. There are so many ex-greats who are still big and recent names. Look at Philip Buchanan, Edgerrin James, Bryant McKinnie, Clinton Portis, Jeremy Shockey. And it's such an interesting group. It's not a judgmental group, it's a constructive group."

Coker believes there remains a misconception that the Hurricanes have dominated for so many years because of their aura and swagger. "It's a little misleading that the swagger won," Coker said. "The swagger was a confidence thing, it was not orchestrated so much. You still have to block and make first downs and tackle, it takes more than swagger. You look back and you see very good players, and that made the swagger effective. They were road warriors, too, and that boded well."

FROM THE BROADCAST BOOTH

Joe Zagacki, long-time Hurricanes' radio broadcaster, provided these memorable tales:

• "After the Hurricanes beat Oklahoma in the 1988 Orange Bowl, the players were celebrating with Coach Jimmy Johnson," Zagacki recalled. "Johnson led them in a dance and chant, 'hit or be hit'. Swaying back and forth he told the players remember the Three P'S. 'We played with poise, we played with pride and when we got hot and tired we pressed on.'

"Then out of the back of the room offensive line coach Tony Wise yelled, 'And one more thing. You guys are tough mother- #@?/##^%!". Of course this was all on the radio and my partner Sonny Hirsch said, 'Well, it is past midnight, so I guess the censors can't get us.'"

• "The week after Miami defeated FSU in Wide Right I in 1991, the Canes traveled to Boston College for a night game. Doug Flutie was there, Tom Coughlin was the head coach. Miami held on for a narrow victory preserving their undefeated season, although the game would eventually cost them an out-right championship [They shared it with Washington].

"After the game I was on the elevator with offensive line coach Art Kehoe and a Boston College supporter started taunting Art by saying, 'You were lucky to get out of this one, buddy boy. One more play, buddy boy, and we would have beat you.' I could see the veins in Art's neck swelling. Just then the doors opened on ground level. Art said, 'What was that about?' I said, 'You should have told him, 'Let me know when you beat the Yankees, buddy boy.' The fan was Joe Morgan, the manager of the Boston Red Sox."

• There are a lot of stories about Miami's 46-3 demolition of third-ranked Texas at the 1991 Cotton Bowl. Craig Erickson threw four touchdown passes and the Hurricanes were penalized 16 times for 202 yards (compared to 68 penalty yards for Texas).

The story that sticks with Zagacki was after the game when center Darren Handy stood at the top of the end zone tunnel as the teams headed for their locker rooms and started yelling at the forlorn Longhorns, "We just kicked your ass for 60 minutes! Do you want to go back out and we'll do all over again?"

WORDS OF WISDOM

Bailey, who played center for Schnellenberger, relates this tale about Hurricanes taking care of Hurricanes, even at 37,000 feet in the sky.

Eric Winston arrived at UM in 2002 as one of the most touted tight ends in the country and left as one of the most touted offensive tackles in the NFL draft. His freshman year as he was walking down the aisle during a flight to a game, Bailey approached him and offered some words of wisdom.

"It was something that had been talked about and I saw," said Bailey, "and Winston is smart enough to do the math (he earned his degree in international finance and marketing in three years). It was a very simple conversation. I told him what I saw and put it on paper for him.

"I said, 'Do you want be a guy who's maybe in the NFL at tight end or go play a marquis position for a decade and half and make $60 million? From borderline to a 10-to-15-year career.'"

Winston made the switch to offensive tackle before his sophomore year. An anterior cruciate ligament injury during his junior season lowered his draft status, but he was selected in the third round by the Houston Texans and started seven games as a rookie.

CHAPTER 10

Back to the Top

FROM SABAN TO COKER

Assistant head coach Art Kehoe is the one link in Miami's program from Saban to Coker and returning to the program under Al Golden. He has learned something from each head coach.

"Each and every coach has been really different as far as their emotional makeup and composure," Kehoe said. "One thing that guided them was that they were organized and had a plan and were efficient. And they didn't let anybody talk them out of it. Each was very stoic and confident, either outwardly or inwardly, and they believed in their coaches and the system.

"You take something from each one. From Schnellenberger you get the edge. In three or four games we are just going to be better prepared and conditioned. In three or four we're going to have to find an edge because we'll be even. We'll have to create turnovers and execute better. And three or four teams will be better, and we'll have to find an edge. It takes everybody to be number one.

Butch Davis

"With Jimmy, his deal was in big bold letters in the locker room: 'POSITIVE MENTAL ATTITUDE PLUS EFFORT EQUALS PERFORMANCE.' They were as big as road signs. No matter how hot it was, in the middle of two- and three-a-days, everyone was complaining. He'd say, 'Yeah, it's hot and miserable, it's easy to put it on autopilot and just punch this practice in. But we're going to find a way to reach down and be positive about each other and get performance. Anybody can be negative. Be positive.'

"Dennis, to me, really emphasized to the players that it was 'your team. When you play the game, let's have some fun and make some plays. We have the system and will make plays. We recruited you to get in big games like this, so go have some fun.' Gary Stevens, his offensive coordinator, would tell the offense, 'Tomorrow we're on national TV against Michigan. People will be turning that tube on because they want to see you guys and want to watch you. You're the show and don't let them down. You've worked your tail off. Now go to bed and dream about making big plays.'

"Butch, when we were on probation, knew we didn't have a chance to win every time out. He said, 'Don't tell me about the Sugar Bowl or national championship, but about the next game. Nothing is more important. Everybody expects Miami to win the national championship, but you can't think that way. You've got to think about the next game. It's like life. Each season is not a destination but a journey. You've got to conquer a journey this week.'

"What intrigues me about Al Golden is his knowledge of history of the University of Miami and how much he's poured himself into what this place all about and the success it has had. I think he understands what Howard and Lou and Jimmy and all the coaches found out, that right in our back yard there are so many good players, and because we branded the last 30 years the brand that is the U we can go out and nab a kid in Texas or Chicago or Massachusetts or Maryland or North Carolina or George. And Al knows that."

EMPHASIZING CHARACTER

Kehoe noted that Butch Davis "was a grinder. But he had some fun. He took over at a time when we were grabbing ourselves with bootstraps, like when Howard and Lou were here. It wasn't a great situation. He just kept saying, 'Just keep doing what we're doing.' The number-one thing that jumps out about Butch—the very first month he was here, he was coming from the NFL, and they do their homework on prospects around the clock. They have more film and more use of it. The first month we sat down and met around the clock and discussed every single player and said, 'Why are we recruiting him? If we had to recruit him again, would we? Who recruited him? How did he do in school? And what was his attitude, and did he come with any luggage or kids out of wedlock?'

"We talked about where we were and what we needed to do to make it better. Who were we going to seek out? We talked to guidance counselors, teachers, security guards, anybody you can come up with. He knew it was in our best interests to get as many opinions as we could. You want to know as much about the product you're buying. Look at the legacy he left—the 19 draft picks in the first round in recent years. A lot were Butch's. Obviously we made some good picks. He derived a lot of his philosophy from Jimmy, but he wanted to find the total type of guys who are at the top of the line in height, weight and speed. And look for playmakers, too.

"I remember looking at Gainesville Buchholz and Gainesville High on film. Clinton Portis moved to running back as a senior, and a lot of people didn't know about him. Someone said, 'Who's that guy? He can play.' And we ended up taking him. And I don't think the Gators were on him that hard even though he was in Gainesville. He was a returning All-State defensive back, and their running back was out with an injury and they needed him.

Larry Coker

"Butch was always coaching the coaches. He wanted us interacting with players, developing relationships with parents and players. Larry carried a lot of that over.

"When we were on probation, and attendance had dwindled from high 50 and low 60 thousands into the 20s and we could only sign nine to 11 recruits, things looked the lowest. But Butch had a plan. He told us to recruit walk-ons, to sell guys on the fact that they could play as young guys. He raised money for the building expansion at the Hecht Athletic Center during the low times. He didn't want any excuses on why we couldn't get it done."

SEMINOLE SPEARING

Each season during Florida State Week, the Hurricane Club of Broward County tries to have Art Kehoe speak at a luncheon. Hurricane radio analyst and former Kehoe teammate Don Bailey recalls what happened one year in the mid-1990s during the NCAA sanctions when Miami wasn't as dominant.

"Everybody wants Art during FSU week," Bailey said. "He got up on the stage and was going through his speech. He had the Seminole spear, which looked like bamboo, something hollow. He got everybody riled up, and at the end of his talk he raised the spear with both hands and was going to break it with his forehead.

"He slams it down on his forehead and it doesn't break. But he almost breaks the bridge of nose, suffers a black eye, swollen nose and a bit of a bruised ego. He didn't fall unconscious but took three steps back. He thought somebody already broke it for him. And, of course, he denied it hurt. But he never did that again."

THE IMMACULATE DEFLECTION

Television replays of the "Hail Flutie" pass that beat the Hurricanes in 1984 have become a staple of college football. The play is part of the lore at the College Football Hall of Fame in South Bend, Indiana; it's inevitably shown every time the teams meet, and it even became part of a television commercial in 2003.

Late in the 2001 season, the Hurricanes produced their own play for the ages. It fittingly happened against Boston College, and it saved a season and a shot at the national championship.

With the Hurricanes clinging to a 12-7 lead in the final minute at Chestnut Hill, Massachusetts, Boston College drove to a first and goal at the Miami nine-yard line. The Hurricanes' 17-game winning streak and No. 1 ranking in the nation clearly was in jeopardy.

Brian St. Pierre then threw a pass intended for Ryan Read, and the ball bounced off the knee of cornerback Mike Rumph and caromed into the hands of Hurricane tackle Matt Walters at the 10. Ed Reed, Miami's All-America strong safety, knew that the six-foot-five, 263-pound Walters didn't have a receiver's speed, so he decided to help out. He snatched the ball from Walters's grasp, nearly lost his balance, regained it and raced 80 yards for Miami's only touchdown in an 18-7 victory.

Luck? A fluke? Or product of an opportunistic defense? Probably all of the above.

"In the red zone they tried to throw a slant," said Rumph. "So when the receiver went outside I was already there. I knelt down to get it and it bounced off my knee. I thought, aww, I missed the play. But when Matt got it, I knew we had the game."

Said Walters: "It took that ball like an hour to fall in my hands. Once it did, I just secured it tight. I was just heading out of bounds and Reed yelled at me, 'Give it to me! Give it to me! I turned to look at him, and I saw it was Reed and let him have it."

Reed said he didn't know why he decided to make the risky move of grabbing the ball from his teammate. "I should have just kneeled and run the clock out. ... I saw he was trying to get out of bounds, but he's a little fat boy."

No Ivory Tower for Shalala

Donna Shalala, who at Wisconsin was the first woman chancellor in the Big Ten and served as U.S. Secretary of Health and Human Services during the Clinton administration, is a sports enthusiast and avid tennis player and golfer. When she accepted the position as president of the University of Miami in 2001, she said she was "looking for a place with a good football team."

At games she'll sit in the president's box for a while, but she enjoys being part of the crowd and sitting among boosters and students.

"I'm happy to go up and sit in the box to do what I have to do for large donors and our trustees for a short period," she said. "But I'm less likely to have fixed tickets than I am to sort of just plunk myself down somewhere and talk to whomever's next to me."

While at Wisconsin (1987-93) she learned that it's best to sit among the students early in the game, before the partying kicks in and they start crowd-surfing people to the top of the stands.

"I decided on that," Shalala said, "once after sitting there in the fourth quarter and someone said, 'Pass her up.'"

When she first sat in the stands at the Orange Bowl, "the students were shocked to see me. Actually they made space for me."

Shalala and Coker lived a charmed 2001 season as the Hurricanes went undefeated and won the national championship game over Nebraska in Miami's first appearance at the Rose Bowl.

"That's about as good as it gets," Shalala said. "When we went to the Rose Bowl they had a luncheon and invited the two presidents of the universities. Nebraska's chancellor got up and thanked 'all the universities that lost so we could be here.' And

I got up and didn't have to thank anyone. It brought down the house. About six teams had to lose for Nebraska to get there."

Refocusing After 9-11

Shortly after the events of 9-11, President Shalala went over to talk to the Hurricanes. "Larry said the team was quite upset," she said. "I remember one of the players, offensive lineman Sherko Haji-Rasouli, was Iranian. I thought he might be feeling the worst. I called him over, and told him I had been on the Peace Corps as a volunteer in Iran [in the early 1960s]. We talked quietly, and I told him I hoped he'd explain to his teammates that not everybody who is Iranian is a Muslim or a terrorist. It was a very unusual moment.

"I told the team that we were going to keep playing. The terrorists wanted to shut us down, but we're not shutting down classrooms or a game. They were focused."

The tragedies had a profound effect on the players, especially when they learned that the mother of freshman linebacker Leon Williams worked in the World Trade Center. Players and team chaplains joined Williams in the locker room that morning to pray as he awaited word on whether she was safe.

It turned out she arrived for work late and got to the building after the tragedy happened and returned home. When she called the football office, there was a sigh of relief among players, and they started clapping and hugging Williams.

Low-Key Impression

It was easy for Donna Shalala to buy into Larry Coker. When she interviewed him for the job in 2001, he didn't come across as a man thinking he was doing the university a favor by taking the job. When she asked him to pretend she was a recruit and sell her on coming to the university, he talked about academics, small classes and graduation rates.

"Larry Coker gave a better description than anyone in the administration," she said. "He talked about small classes, talked about the beautiful campus and diversity.

"I interviewed him at the Four Seasons in Washington, D.C. No one knew what Larry looked like. There must have been 20 reporters in the lobby, and they recognized me but not him. He's low key, doesn't have a big ego and is competent. He wanted the job and is smart.

"There's a discipline to him that I recognized. Great coaches are well organized. All great coaches are.

"He is actually more animated than he seems. It's a kind of discipline. He can be very funny."

Coker recalled that "We had an interesting meeting. Of course, I was very nervous. She's such a terrific communicator, she made it very relaxed."

SIDELINE COACHING

Edwin Pope, the longtime *Miami Herald* sports editor who has covered every Hurricane team since the mid-1950s, has known the 14 head coaches during that span well. His reflections on a few:

"I'd say that Butch Davis was one of the most relentlessly upbeat coaches I've ever been around. I asked him once, 'Why did you come to Miami?' He said, 'Well, I was an assistant here and I wanted to be a head coach. I had a possible chance to coach the Oakland Raiders. They didn't offer me the job, but owner Al Davis talked to me. Another reason was I wanted to get away from Barry Switzer at the Cowboys. What a mess the

Cowboys are. Barry's so often not around when they need him. One draft day he called from hundreds of miles away.'

"Butch had a way of projecting certain scenarios that turned out not to exist. Sometimes his imagination ran rampant. I have to say this about Butch: I thought Butch was one of the most decent people I've ever met. He not only was a great recruiter of talent but a great recruiter of people with character. He pretty much straightened out the mess Dennis left when things were pretty much going to pot, no pun intended. For that I admire him. I didn't care for him much as a sideline coach on the day of a game. He exhibited some panic. I've felt a coach's demeanor is contagious. He had a habit of showing desperation, and I didn't think it helped the team much. Overall he did a fantastic job taking Miami out of a ditch, and he was a credit to UM.

"I thought Dennis Erickson was an excellent sideline coach. He was on top of everything. At his best he is a heck of a football coach. Coker is such an entirely different creature, so different from the others. I've never known a coach with less self-importance. It seems to be a virus for guys who are assistants who become head coaches. They can be forthright as assistants, but when they become head coaches, most of them become devious, conniving. Their whole demeanor changes. They become very selfish. Maybe it's a matter of survival. Larry Coker is one of a very few head coaches who didn't become a much different kind of person after he became head coach. I understand that Butch's last year of recruiting in 2000-2001, he didn't make a single home visit, and Larry made a lot of them. Larry locked them up. And about a dozen of those guys became pretty good players. Coker nearly won the national title again in 2002, losing to Ohio State in two overtimes at the Fiesta Bowl on a controversial call. As UM's record slipped to 11-2, 9-3, 7-6, and bowl berths tumbled from the Orange Bowl Classic to the MPC Computers Bowl in Boise, Idaho, he was dismissed in 2006.

PATIENCE PAYS OFF

After 22 years as an assistant coach at the collegiate level, Larry Coker's patience and perseverance paid off when he was named head coach of the Hurricanes in 2001. A little inspiration from his wife, Dianna, paid off, too.

During the hectic five days between the announcement of Butch Davis leaving for the Cleveland Browns to the promotion of Coker to replace him, Coker opened his briefcase and saw a note written by his wife on a yellow pad. It was from Psalm 40 in the Bible and said: "Wait patiently."

"Boy, that says it right there," Coker recalled. "Get back to business, go to work and wait patiently."

RETIRE UNDEFEATED?

Pope relates this story that Coker loves to tell: The coach was home in the off season after winning the national title his first season and his wife, Dianna, said:

"You know, Larry, have you thought about retiring undefeated?"

"No, I hadn't," Larry replied.

"Well, why don't you think about it?" Dianna said. "We could do it financially."

"I just got this huge raise," the coach said.

"You know, Larry," Dianna said, "those boys really need you."

CHAPTER 11

Transition and NFL Greatness

GIVE ME YOUR CELL PHONES

Stephen Sapp, professor and chairman of the Department of Religious Studies at UM, has known Randy Shannon since Shannon was a linebacker for the Hurricanes from 1985-88. Having served as honorary faculty coach several times, Sapp followed Shannon's career as a UM assistant coach, defensive coordinator and head coach, from student to player disciplinarian to jolting UM's Board of Trustees.

"I taught Randy when he was an undergrad in a 200-level course of about 30 students," Sapp said. "He was faithful in attendance, participated fairly regularly, and did decent work (it was clear he at least took the course seriously). Interestingly, I do not recall the speech issues that plagued him with the media when he was head coach. And he was of course (as you can imagine) a stunningly impressive physical specimen! We stayed in touch over the years, bumping into each other occasionally, and he always greeted me with, 'Hey, Doc! How's my favorite UM prof?' When he was linebackers coach, I had the pleasure of being selected as Honorary Faculty Defensive Coach for the FSU game, and he immediately took me under his wing and shepherded me through the team meetings, workouts, and other activities. After he became defensive coordinator, I had several players in the big Religion 101 class in the Learning Center, and it was obvious from the beginning they were not taking the course seriously, sitting in the far back corner, talking and laughing, and fooling around with their phones.

"I spoke to them about it but nothing changed, so I called Randy and told him they were going to have problems come test time because obviously they were not paying attention. I expected him to speak to them at practice about it, but when I arrived at the classroom the next class day, Randy was standing outside the room and told me he would handle the problem. I'll never forget the look on the faces of those guys when they walked up and saw Coach Shannon standing there with his arm around my shoulders! He looked at them with that 'Randy stare' and said calmly, 'Give me your phones, right now.' They didn't hesitate, and after he had collected them he ushered them into the room down to the second row and sat down behind them, where he stayed for the entire class. And that's where they sat the rest of the semester, attentive and phoneless!"

Bailey added, "That has happened more than once. And that to me that's the side of Randy Shannon and the heart and soul of Randy Shannon that not enough people know."

Sapp's other favorite Shannon story concerns the day he was introduced to the Board of Trustees Executive Committee as the new head coach.

"As Faculty Senate Chair at the time he was hired, I had the pleasure of being in on his final interview with the President and Provost," Sapp recalled. "The meeting was in H-100 of the Bank United Center, and Pascal Goldschmidt was giving a report on the med school when Randy was brought in. President Shalala interrupted the meeting and said that she wanted them to meet our new head football coach, who had lots of things to do and couldn't stay very long. She introduced Randy, and just as he began to speak one of the Trustees' cell phone rang. Without missing a beat, Randy looked straight at him, stretched out his hand toward him, and said with an absolutely straight face, 'Phone, right here, right now.'

"What had been a quiet room got even quieter, and when the Trustee just stared at him, Randy said calmly, 'That's my rule. When a phone goes off in a meeting, I get it until the next meeting.' He waited exactly the right amount of time to let the shock and perplexity build and then, flashing his brilliant smile, said, "But you didn't know my rule so I guess you can keep it... this time!'

"I remember thinking to myself, 'He absolutely has them in his back pocket now.' Would that he could have won a few more games more quickly!"

Hurricanes' broadcaster, Brian London, added, "When you think about the totality of the program, Randy really improved the academics and discipline. Off the field he helped the program, and he doesn't get enough credit for that."

Reproduced courtesy of The University of Miami Athletics Department

TRICKING THE SEMINOLES

Shannon didn't mind gambling or taking chances in a game. Before the 2007 meeting with Florida State at Tallahassee, he said to the Voice of the Hurricanes Joe Zagacki, "If you see Francesco Zampogna in the game we're going to fake the field goal. The holder is going to flip it over his shoulder and Z will throw it."

Sure enough, midway through the third quarter Zampogna came on to attempt a field goal. And Zagacki announced, "Some trickery might be involved." The holder flipped the ball to Zampogna, who threw a pass to tight end DajLeon Farr for a touchdown, giving Miami a 24-23 lead. The Hurricanes went on to win 37-29.

Zagacki recalls that after the game he said to standout junior defensive end Calais Campbell, "You have to come back for another year."

Replied Campbell, "I love college and would love to stay, but my family has been poor our entire lives and they want me to earn some money."

Campbell turned pro, was drafted in the second round by the Arizona Cardinals and played in Super Bowl XLIII.

COACH WHO?

Anthony Chickillo was a five-star recruit out of Tampa's Alonso High School. His grandfather, Nick, had been a first-team All-American as a two-way lineman in the early 1950s for the Hurricanes, and his father had been a standout defensive tackle for the Hurricanes from 1979-82. Both played in the NFL.

But there were concerns as to whether Anthony would become the first third-generation Hurricane. After Shannon was dismissed following the 2010 season, UM director of athletics

Kirby Hocutt called Anthony and encouraged him to be patient as the school searched for a new head coach.

"He was calling me and kept telling me that 'Just stick with us, we're going to get a big-time head coach that everybody knows.' When I heard we were going to get Jon Gruden [who coached the Tampa Bay Buccaneers to the Super Bowl title], I thought, wow, that's going to be awesome. So when I found out it was Coach Golden I'm like, now who's this guy? I was thinking to myself.

"And then the very next day Coach Golden and [defensive coordinator Mark] D'Onofrio knocked on my door. After that we sat down at my house and I remember being so impressed with the plan Coach Golden had that he talked about in my living room, what he wants to do here at Miami. There was no doubt in my mind that he was going to do it. That's when I was sold on Coach Golden. He was the right guy.

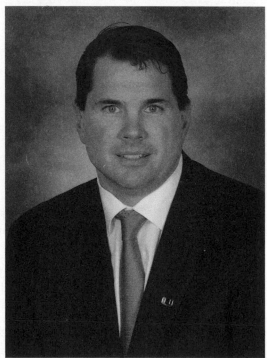

Reproduced courtesy of The University of Miami Athletics Department

"My dad likes coach Golden and coach D'Onofrio. He likes the plan Coach Golden has and says he reminds him a little bit of a mix of Coach Schnellenberger with Jimmy Johnson in him. Two guys he definitely respects, Coach Schnellenberger being his coach and Coach Johnson pretty much being a guy everyone loves."

TWO ACRES AND A BALL

As Golden's first season at UM unfolded in 2011, he encouraged the Hurricanes to look at football in simple terms: two acres and a ball.

"Coach Golden always says when we're going to play at a big place in front of a big crowd, just think in your head it's two acres and a ball," said defensive end Anthony Chickillo. "That's all there is. Just like you've been doing it your whole life. When we're going to the big places like Florida State and Virginia Tech he says, 'Two acres and a ball.' Then you think about that. He says it a lot throughout team meetings. It always comes up."

Cornerback Brandon McGee added, "I think the entire team bought into that mentality. Books and balls, that's all you have to worry about."

Long-time offensive line coach and former UM player Art Kehoe noted, "The point of it is, don't get caught up in crowd or stadium or atmosphere. Whether you're practicing or playing in a game, it's two acres and ball, 100 yards and two end zones. What it comes down to is, make decisions on who wins and loses. Who owns those two acres? There might be a melee in that corner of the stadium, cannons might be going off and nude women screaming and yelling. The bottom line is, what you have control of is 11 of us and 11 of them, and we need to protect the ball if we've got it and get the ball if we don't' have it.

"I like it. It's cool, it's what he's all about. Good stuff. He's funny, too, laughs a lot. Even when I played for Howard

Schnellenberger, we'd laugh but not as much. He had that stern voice and was so businesslike. With Al you know how he feels. He likes players to have fun."

Golden showed that after the Hurricanes failed to score a touchdown but still won 6-3 at South Florida. "After the game and they closed the locker room door, you see Coach Golden in the middle of the whole team and jumping around and enjoying the victory with us," said McGee. "When you have a coach that remembers how it used to feel when he played, you can relate to him a lot more. He's jumping around yelling, 'It's great to be a Miami Hurricane!' He was leading the chant. That makes the game fun and makes winning fun and makes playing fun. You just want to go out and play for your coach and your teammates."

SOME HOWARD, SOME JIMMY

Former Hurricane center and long-time radio analyst Don Bailey has been involved with the program since the late 1970s. In Golden he sees a lot of Schnellenberger and Johnson.

"The first thing that comes to mind when I think of Al Golden," Bailey said, "is that they say lightning doesn't strike twice in the same place. But I think it might have for UM. And a lot of things have got to fall in place, but we are fortunate to have a combination of Howard Schnellenberger and Jimmy Johnson all in one.

"You have the psychological approach, charismatic approach and competitive approach of Jimmy Johnson with a vision and the organizational skills and sheer determination to win of Howard Schnellenberger. And to think you can get a guy this day and age of this caliber, Miami is very fortunate. I think he's as good as advertised.

"Things are a lot different. Parity has kicked in. There are seven schools instead of three in Florida playing football. There's no more secret about the talent in South Florida, no fear to recruit the inner city. A lot of things have made it more difficult to be coach at the University of Miami.

"The key is the time, the era that we're in and the understanding of the time that it takes. It's an open market. There are 380 kids that Miami, Florida and FSU used to pick through that many are now playing at Florida International, Florida Atlantic, Central Florida and South Florida. Probably 80 percent of those rosters are Florida kids. Forget Alabama getting Trent Richardson (of Pensacola) and almost winning the Heisman Trophy."

Most Impressive Run in Sports?

In addition to the 58-game home winning streak in the Orange Bowl and the 33-game winning streak from 2000 to 2002, there's another streak that arguably is the most impressive in modern sports: For 149 consecutive NFL regular-season weekends, a span of nearly nine years, at least one former Hurricane scored a touchdown.

It began on Week 15 in December, 2002, when rookie running back Clinton Portis scored four touchdowns for the Denver Broncos. He became the youngest player in NFL history (21 years, 105 days) to score four touchdowns in a game, and he started the Hurricanes' NFL scoring streak that continued until November 22, 2011.

The streak was discovered by ProCanes.com, verified by the Elias Sports Bureau and dissected in detail by the Miami Herald. It included 661 touchdowns scored by 33 former Hurricanes.

On two occasions no Hurricane scored until Monday Night Football. Bubba Franks of the Green Bay Packers kept it alive with 4:21 to go in the fourth quarter in Week 4 of 2003, and Santana Moss came through in Week 2 of 2005.

There were long touchdowns, including an NFL record 108-yard interception return by Ed Reed of the Baltimore Ravens. There were wild celebrations in the end zone, such as the acrobatic routine by Antrel Rolle of the Arizona Cardinals after two interceptions returned for scores. And there was a somber one when Portis raised his jersey to reveal a t-shirt memorial to his former UM and Washington Redskins team-mate Sean Taylor, who was murdered the week before the game.

"When you turn on *SportsCenter* every night, you don't want to be the one Hurricane left out," Portis said. "It seems like there is always at least one highlight, if not all of them, that involves a UM player. With so many stars in the NFL, it's almost impossible for this streak not to happen. One guy can have an off day, but what are the odds all of us will? Not likely."

Reed, who is responsible for 11 of the touchdowns, said: "We knew when we chose UM that it was the gateway to the NFL. We were competing against future pros every day at practice and working out with NFL guys in the off-season. We all pay attention when a UM guy scores. If you're not playing with one, you're playing against one, or seeing one on the TV highlights. There are a lot of us out there."

During Week 6 in 2005, Hurricanes scored ten touchdowns, the most during the streak. Three were produced by Edgerrin James, two by Moss and Vinny Testaverde, and one each by Willis McGahee, Reggie Wayne, and Jeremy Shockey.

Then there was Santana Claus. On Christmas Eve, 2005, Redskins kicker John Hall walked into the locker room wearing a Santa Claus outfit. "Santana Claus," he joked in regard to teammate Santana Moss, who had scored three touchdowns in a 35-20 victory over the New York Giants. One came on a dazzling 72-yard catch.

Portis, who also scored in that game, said Moss developed his skills at UM by playing Frisbee with a dog.

"He used to catch that Frisbee all the time." Portis said. "He'd outrun the dog, jump up and catch the Frisbee."

The least heralded Hurricane to score? Probably Nick Luchey. His name is not even in the school's record books. He was Nick Williams when he played for UM from 1995-98. During the 2002 NFL season he changed his surname to Luchey to honor his biological father.

On Dec. 22, 2002, after spending most of his time on the scout team and not carrying the ball in the first 14 games, Luchey came off the bench for the 1-13 Cincinnati Bengals and scored two touchdowns in the fourth quarter.

The streak ended on a combination of bad breaks and injuries. Kellen Winslow, Jr., caught a touchdown pass for the Tampa Bay Bucs but was called for pushing off on Sam Shields, a former Hurricane. Ray Lewis, Roscoe Parrish and Moss were sidelined because of injuries. Andre Johnson, Jimmy Graham and Reggie Wayne were out due to a bye week. Frank Gore carried 24 times for 88 yards but no touchdown. Devin Hester had five punt or kickoff returns but didn't score. Greg Olsen, Shockey and McGahee didn't score.

Leading scorers during the streak were Portis and Wayne, with 70 each. McGahee was next with 63, followed by Johnson, 52; Moss, 52; James, 49, and Gore, 45.

Most of the players who scored were first-round draft picks. For 14 consecutive years (1995-2008) at least one Hurricane was selected in the first round. Miami holds the record for most players picked in the first round of a single draft, six in 2004, and the most in a two-year period (11 in 2003-2004), most in a three-year period (15, 2002-2004) and most in a four-year period (19, 2001-2004).

The 149-week streak probably will not be surpassed. The Elias Sports Bureau reported that when it ended, the next longest belonged to the University of Pittsburgh: 12 weeks.

"It's living, breathing proof that Miami accumulated some of the best talent in the history of the game," said Bailey. "It's almost incomprehensible."